99

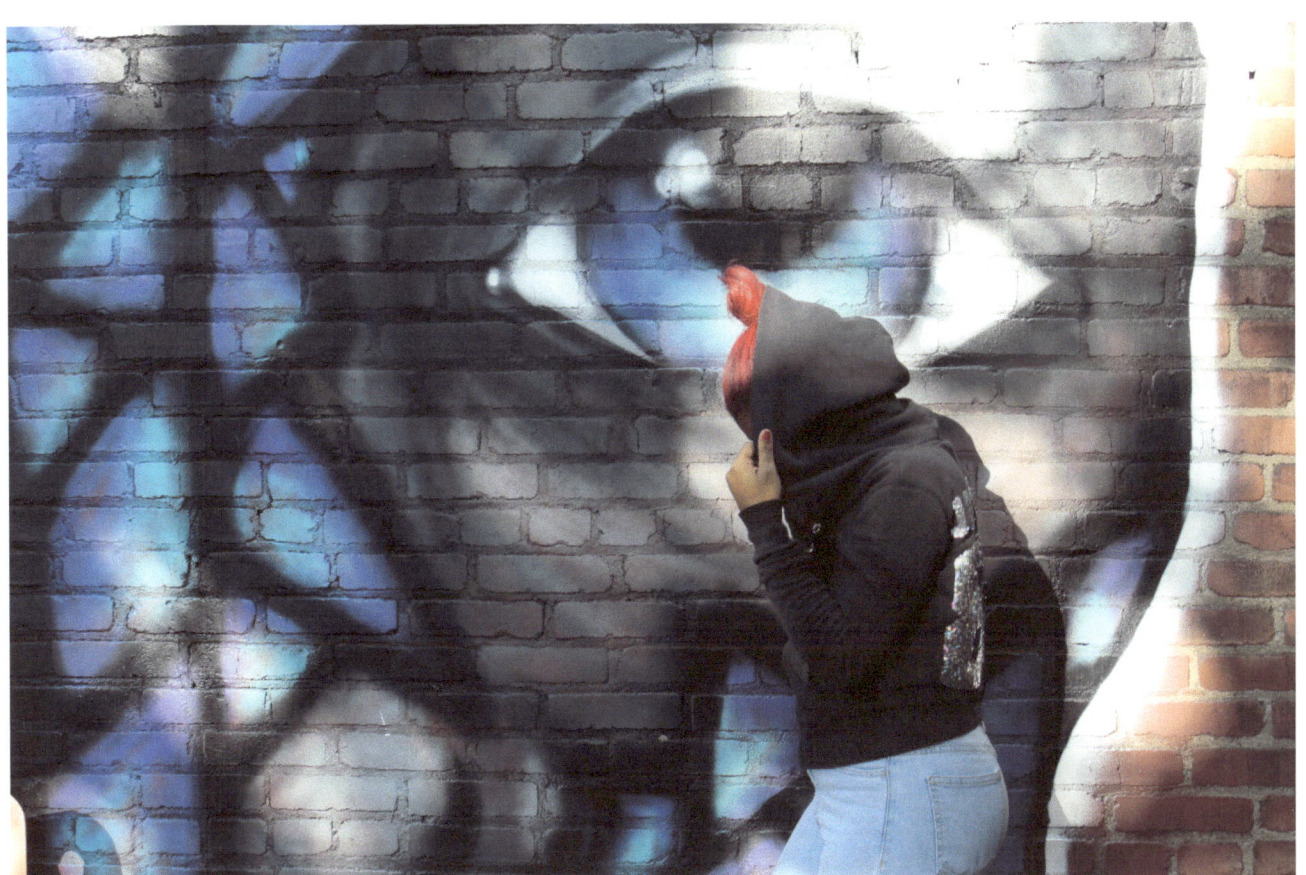

NEW YORK, 2017

* This book was pieced together from a journal I have kept while attending public highschool. All content has been left in its original written text (including spelling, grammar, and the dates in which they were written).

- This is dedicated to the real!!!

40.811° N,

73.9965° W

- Harlem, NY

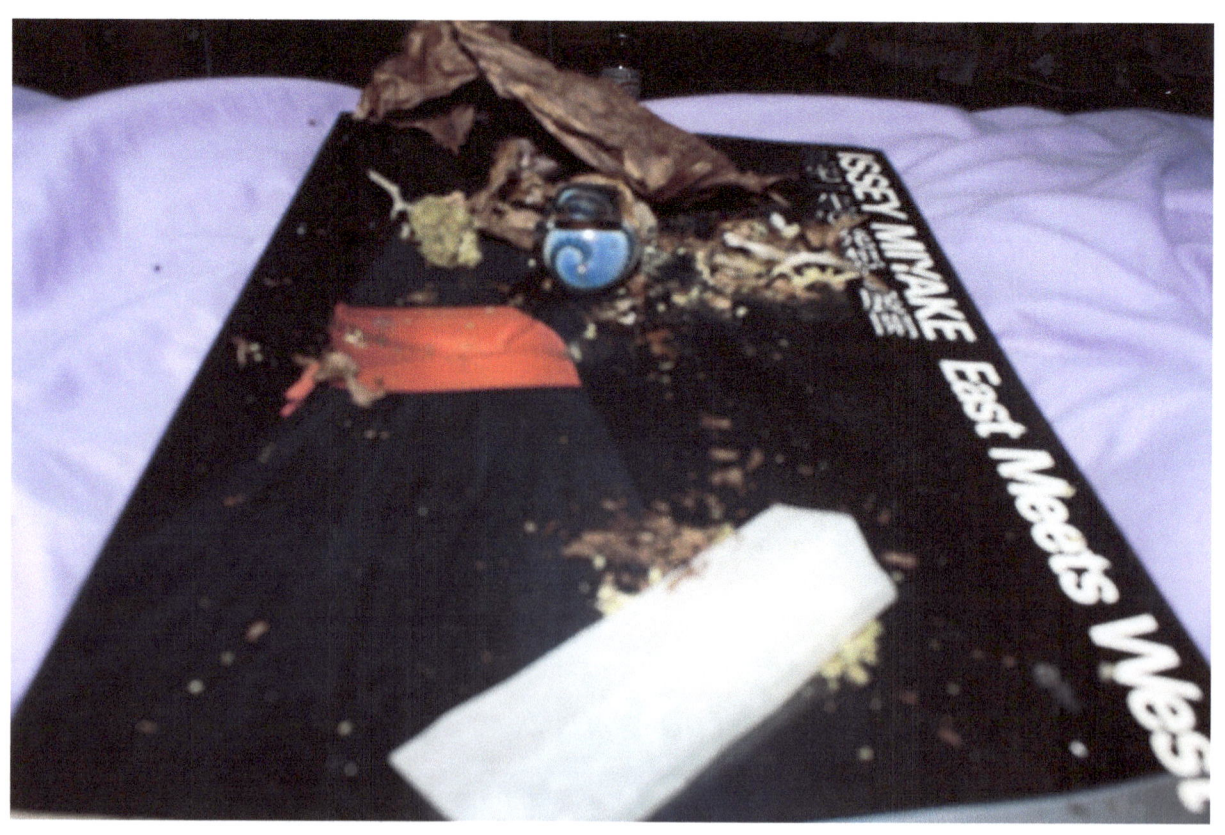

SC (Cyph) Playlist

1. All Alone - Mia Moore

2. Pull Up – Summer

3. Took Time – Dex

4. Gucci please – Gucci

5. My Love – Majid & Drake

6. Go away- Crillz

7. No Heart – 21

8. Broccoli – baby & yatchy

9. Sauce – TRAPFONEE

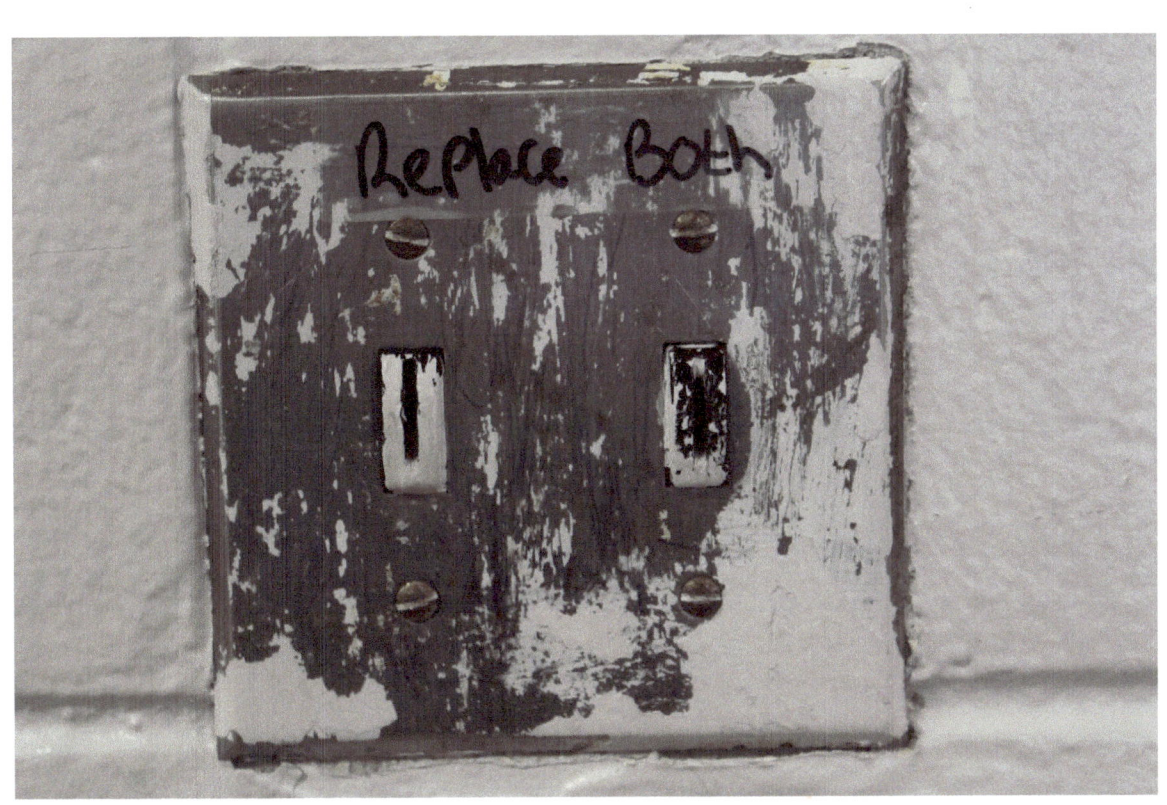

Rainbow measurement lab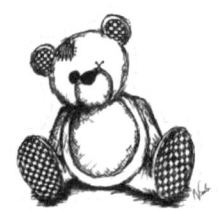

Hypothesis: I predicted each of the test tubes would turn a different color of the rainbow.

Objectives:

To develop skills measuring chemicals with a graduated cylinder.

To practice using the metric system.

To memorize the name of beakers, flasks, graduated cylinders and test tubes.

To test precision and ability to follow directions.

To practice lab safety procedures.

Materials:

- 6 test tubes

Test tube holders

Labels for the test tubes

1 test tube stand

1 pipette

1 glass stirring rod

An 200-400 mL beaker for rinse

A 200-400 mL beaker for waste water

50 mL graduated cylinder

10 mL graduated cylinder

Procedure:

Part 1:

Label 6 test tubes

Fill one of your beakers approximately half full with tap water

The second beaker is for contaminated waste water, from the rinse

Rinse the graduated cylinders and pipettes between all uses.

Into test tube A, measure 26 mL of RED liquid, using the glass stirring rod to prevent drips.

Into test tube C, measure 18 mL of YELLOW liquid, using the glass stirring rod to prevent drips.

Into test tube E, measure 22 mL of BLUE liquid, using the glass stirring rod to prevent drip

Part 2:

From test tube C, measure 4 mL and pour into test tube D.

From test tube E, measure 7 mL and pour into test tube D. swirl.

From test tube E, measure 4 mL and pour into test tube F.

From test tube A, measure 7 mL and pour into test tube F.Swirl.

From test tube A, measure 8 mL and pour into test tube B.

From test tube C, Measure 3 mL and pour into test tube B. swirl.

Record your results in data table.

Add 5 drops of hydrochloric acid to each test tube. Note any changes.

Clean up.

Results:

6

Test tubes	Measurements	color before HCA	Color after HCA
A	26 ml	Red	N/a
C & D	4 ml	Yellow	Yellow
C	18 ml	Yellow	N/a
E & D	7 ml	Yellow	Red
E	22 ml	Blue	N/a
E & F	4 ml	Yellow	Yellow
A & F	7 ml	Yellow	Orange
A & B	8 ml	Yellow	Yellow
C & B	3 ml	Yellow	Orange

Analysis:

It is important to follow directions exactly because your using acid and it can be unsafe if you mix the wrong things.

2 ways to get exact measurements are to use droppers and a scale.

The Two most important objectives are to test precision and practice lab safety procedures.

A reason you might have slightly different amounts in each is because your mixing tubes with different amounts of liquid; The 5 drops of HCA also change the measurements because when using a dropper the drops are not exact.

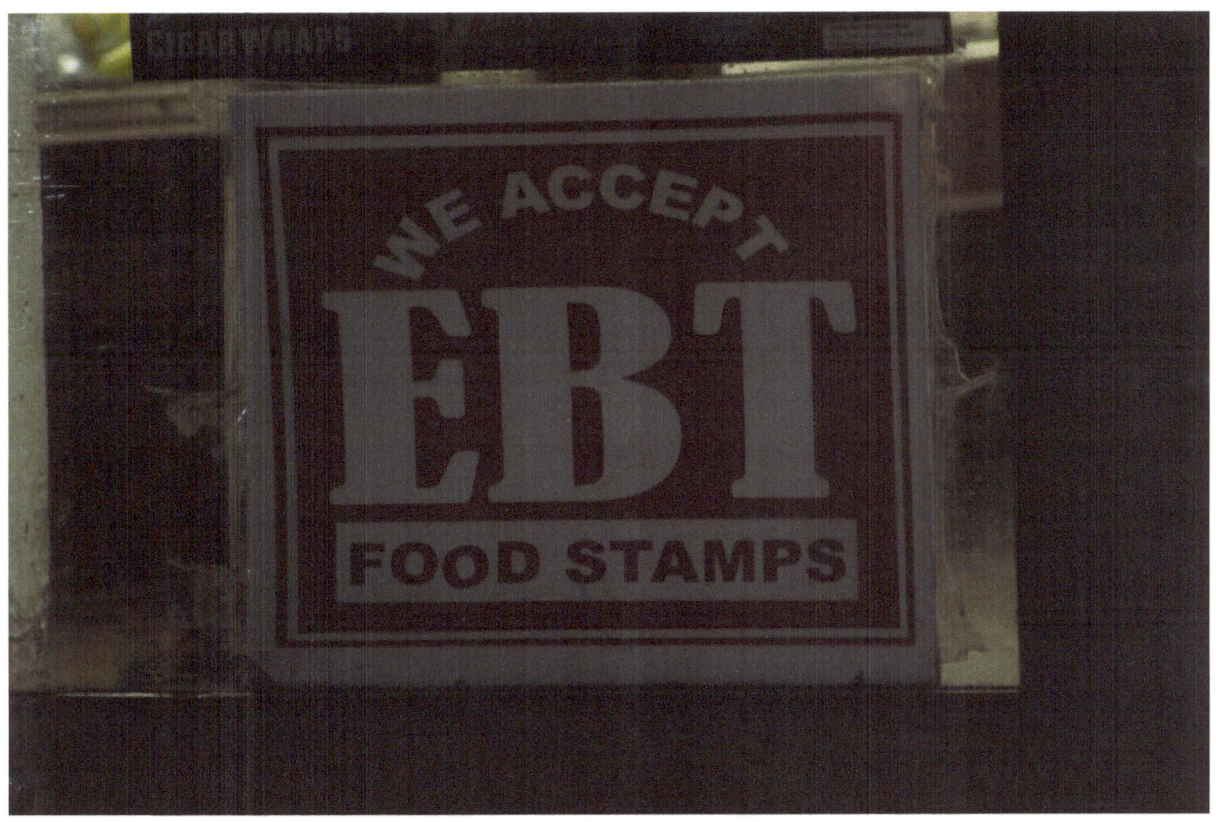

"An epidemic worst then any plaque that human kind has ever seen, has been raging for centuries. It is the "Don't Want" epidemic. "

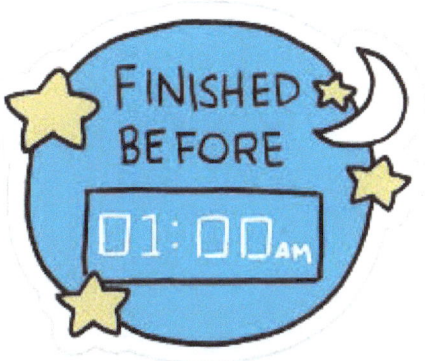

Question:

If you could end one world problem what would it be?

Answer:

No questions asked, I would end world hunger. That is one of the most stupid problems we should have in the world. Food can be grown, preserved, shipped and transported in multiple ways yet there are people who are dying from a lack of food. I love food, I love to eat, I love to cook, I love everything that comes along with food so it makes me sad that everyone cant enjoy food as much as me. You could walk out of your house and get hit by a bus, get cancer and drop dead, have a stroke, etc. dying from a lack of food just seems like the most outrageous way to die. I know it sounds cliche and I know that I cannot feed every starving child in the world but I want to implement home growing food around the world. There are parts of the world where the weather is warm all year round and rainfall is consistent, making home gardening easily achievable.

Describe energy

- it can never be created or destroyed

- It always has been everything that ever existed.

- It is moving through, into and out of form.

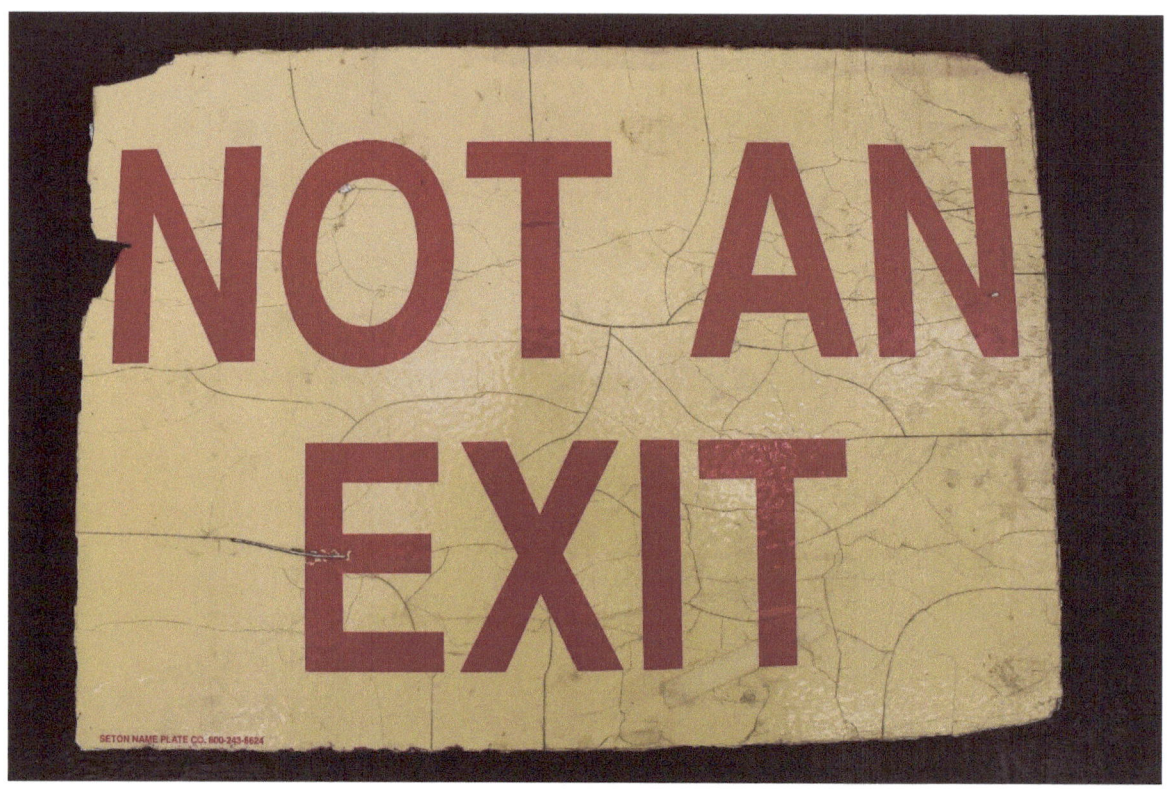

- You are energy and energy is you.

- Less complaining, more doing.

  - Complaining = The transfer of negative energy

  - Doing = The transfer of positive energy

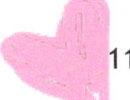

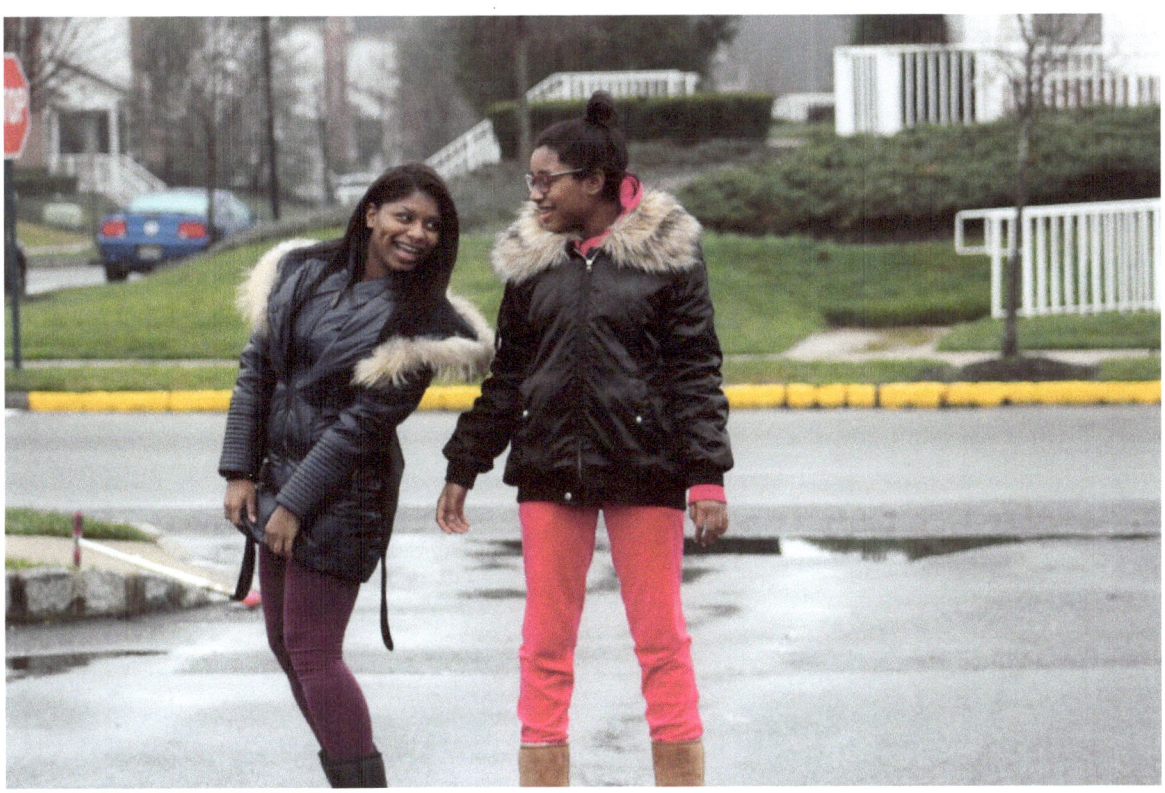

"The power of love is the highest frequency you can emit."

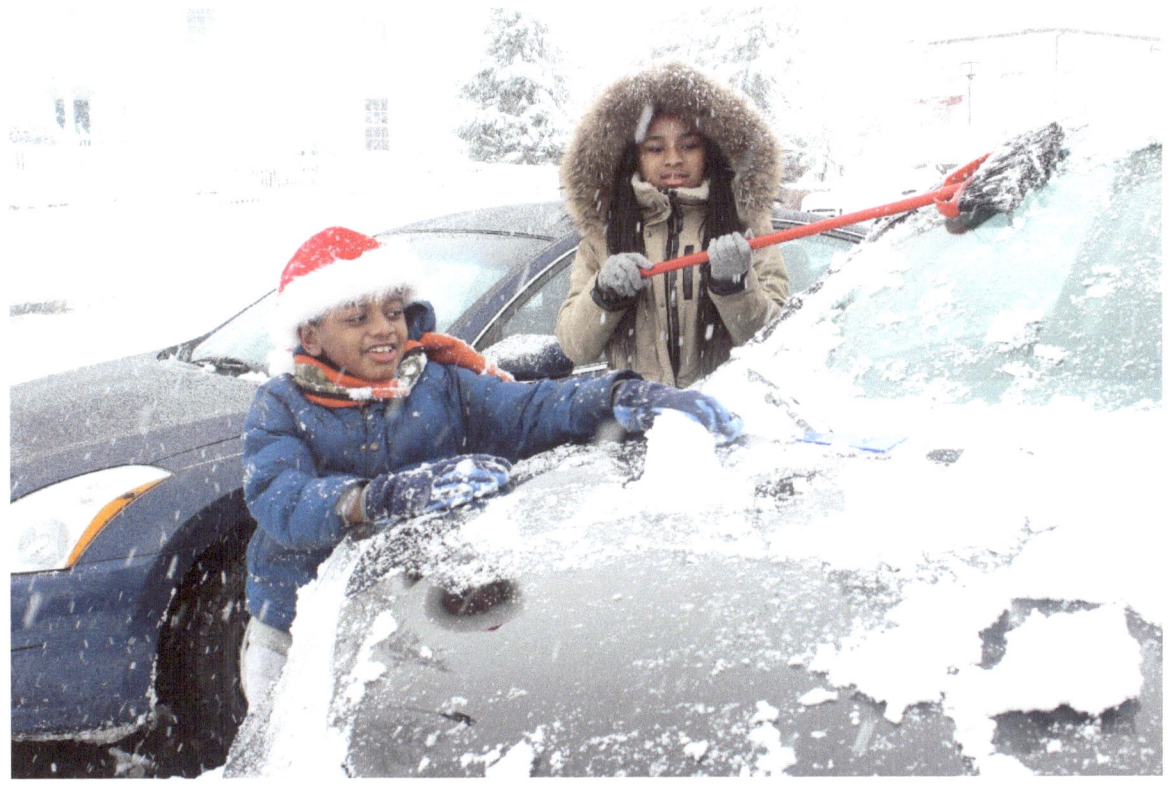

Question: What was the hardest part about growing up in Harlem?

Answer: The hardest part of growing up in Harlem was not understanding the cultural devision that very much still exists. I lived on 116th street and 7th avenue on the upper west side of manhattan also known as Harlem; I could either walk outside and see white people holding hands or see Crack heads sharing cheap liquor. I went to school in downtown manhattan, in a primarily white school on 79th street where every kid came to school with a packed lunch box, my friends in my neighborhood didn't own lunch boxes; They were lucky if they came home to dinner on the stove. Every morning I would go next door from my apartment to a little restaurant called the "Japs" which could hold maybe 20 people on a crowded morning. I would get a cup of grits with American cheese with corn beef hash and I swore it was the best meal of my day even though it cost like $3 dollars. I had a lunch box packed every day for snack like Sarah and James but I also ate $3 grits with Mira and Daquan every morning. I remember going to school and all my friends lived in these huge brown stones where they didn't share a room with siblings and they had these huge birthday parties because their parents could afford them. My friends who lived in my neighborhood didn't have huge brownstones they had bunk beds and they didn't get huge birthday parties they had "Birthday outfits" because thats all their families could afford. I was too "black" for the White kids and too "white" for the black kid which I was constantly reminded of; My neighborhood friends all made fun of the way I spoke, the vocabulary i used that they couldn't understand, my interests in education and my disinterest in breaking the rules. My white friends (although they will never admit it) disproved of the hip hop music I sang, didn't understand why i didn't wet my hair at the pool and were simply conflicted with why we lived different lives yet lived in such close proximity. I lived in the center of Manhattan amongst the poorest of the poor and the richest of the rich.

Him: Come down stairs.

Me: No.

Him: come down stairs, I'm not playing with you.

Me: *comes downstairs*

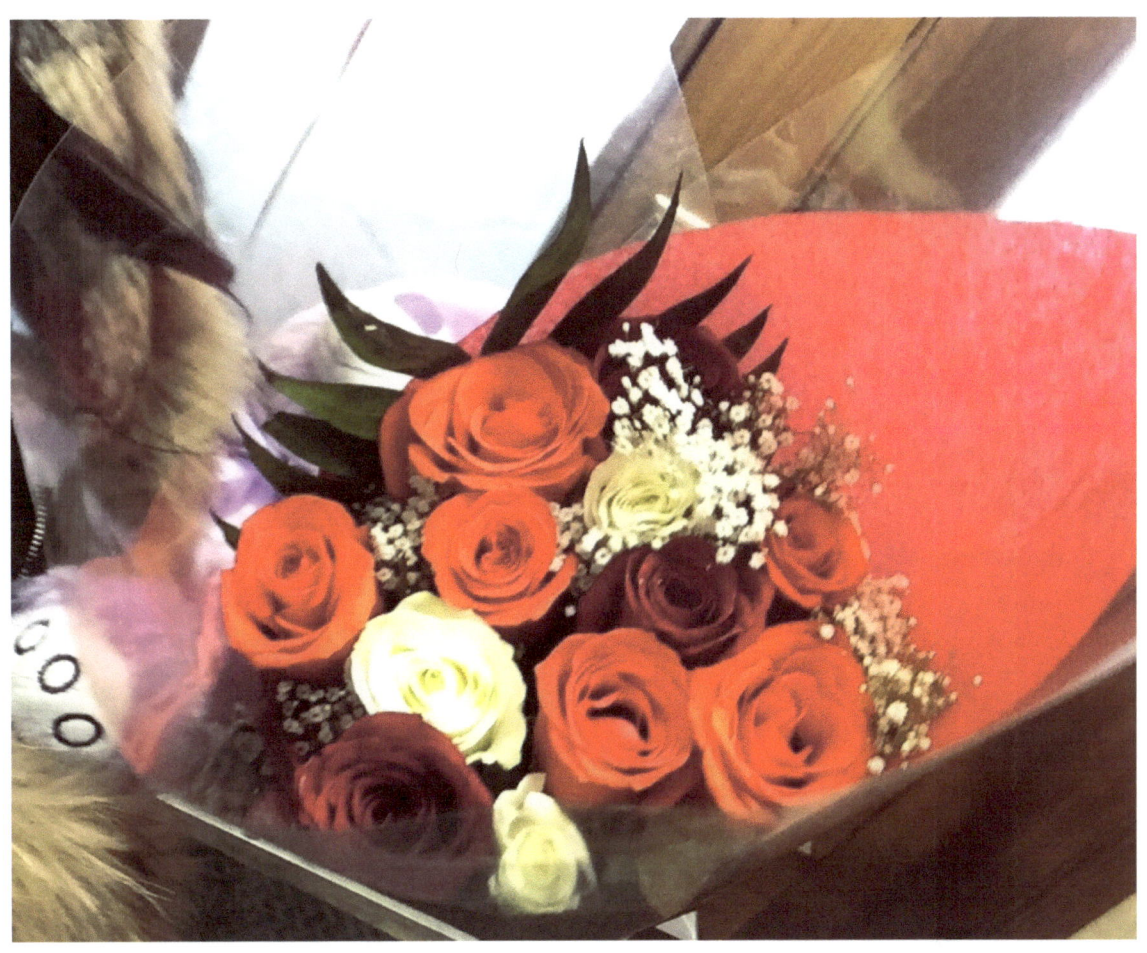

-February 14th 2015

Question: If you could end one world problem what would it be?

Answer: No questions asked, I would end world hunger. That is one of the most stupid problems we should have in the world. Food can be grown, preserved, shipped and transported in multiple ways yet there are people who are dying from a lack of food. I love food, I love to eat, I love to cook, I love everything that comes along with food so it makes me sad that everyone cant enjoy food as much as me. You could walk out of your house and get hit by a bus, get cancer and drop dead, have a stroke, etc. dying from a lack of food just seems like the most outrageous way to die. I know it sounds cliche and I know that I cannot feed

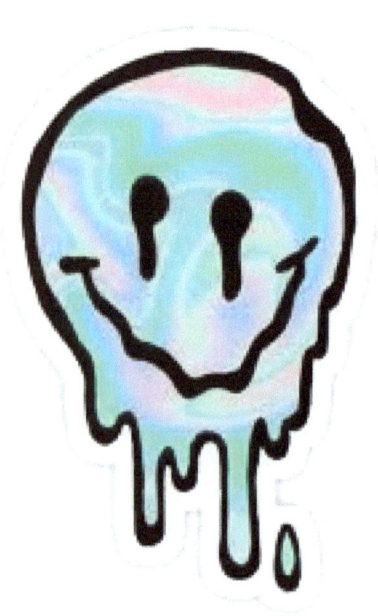

every starving child in the world but I want to implement home growing food around the world. There are parts of the world where the weather is warm all year round and rainfall is consistent, making home gardening easily achievable.

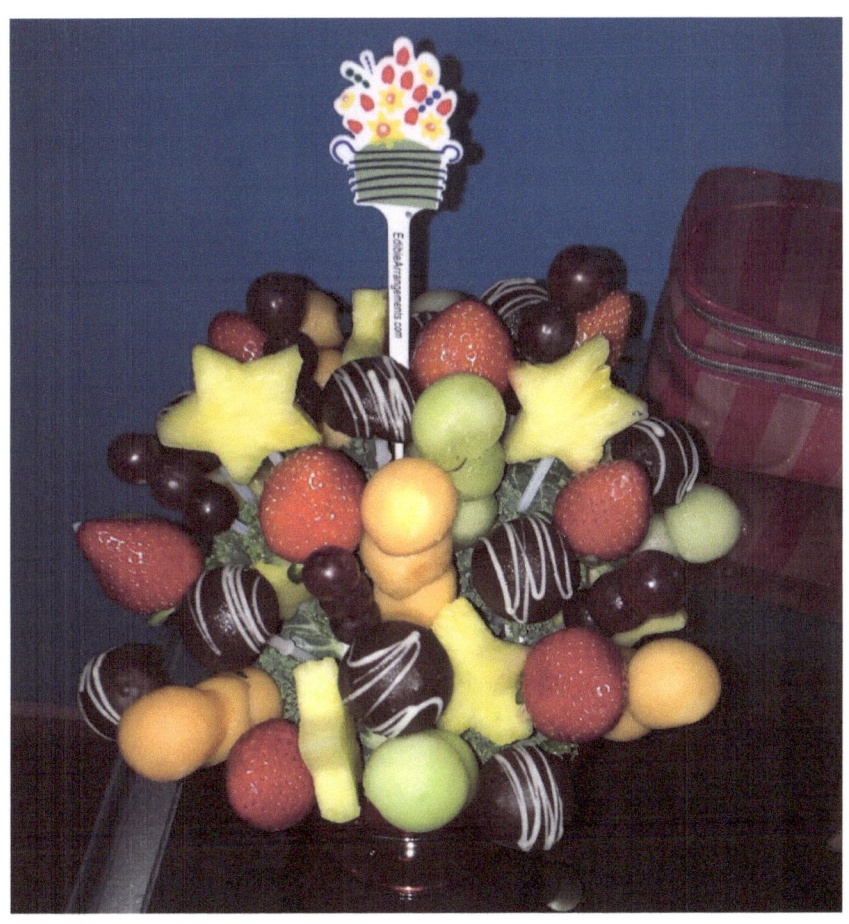

- February 24th 2015

"~~Even you being stuck in the middle of the woods couldn't stop me from surprising you lol. Happy Birthday mi amor! I love you unconditionally, your fat ass always eating so take these fruits to nourish your body lol 9.9.12~~" – A hood Love note

Q: What is your opinion on the weed epidemic?

A: I am fully supporting the proclaimed " Weed Antics". It is simple. When I was 16 I was in a bad accident and was prescribed pain pills, I started smoking weed substituting the pills. Why would I take pills that were making me sick, lose weight, sleep and be extremely moody when I can smoke weed and be just as relieved of pain. Smoking weed is not only a pain reliever but a social activity that I enjoy. It is a reason for people to meet and chill on a Tuesday for no reason, it makes people want to get up out of the bed and go communicate with other people. Migraines are horrible and anyone who hasn't experienced them cannot dismiss the concept of Medical Marijuana!

#GucciForPresident16

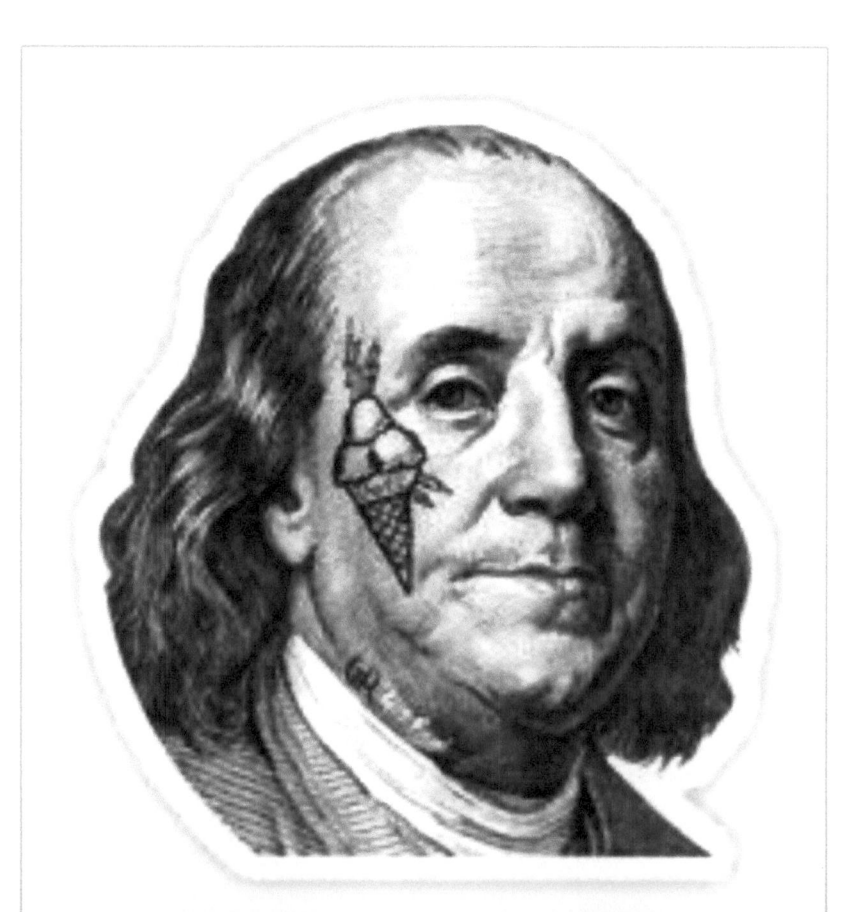

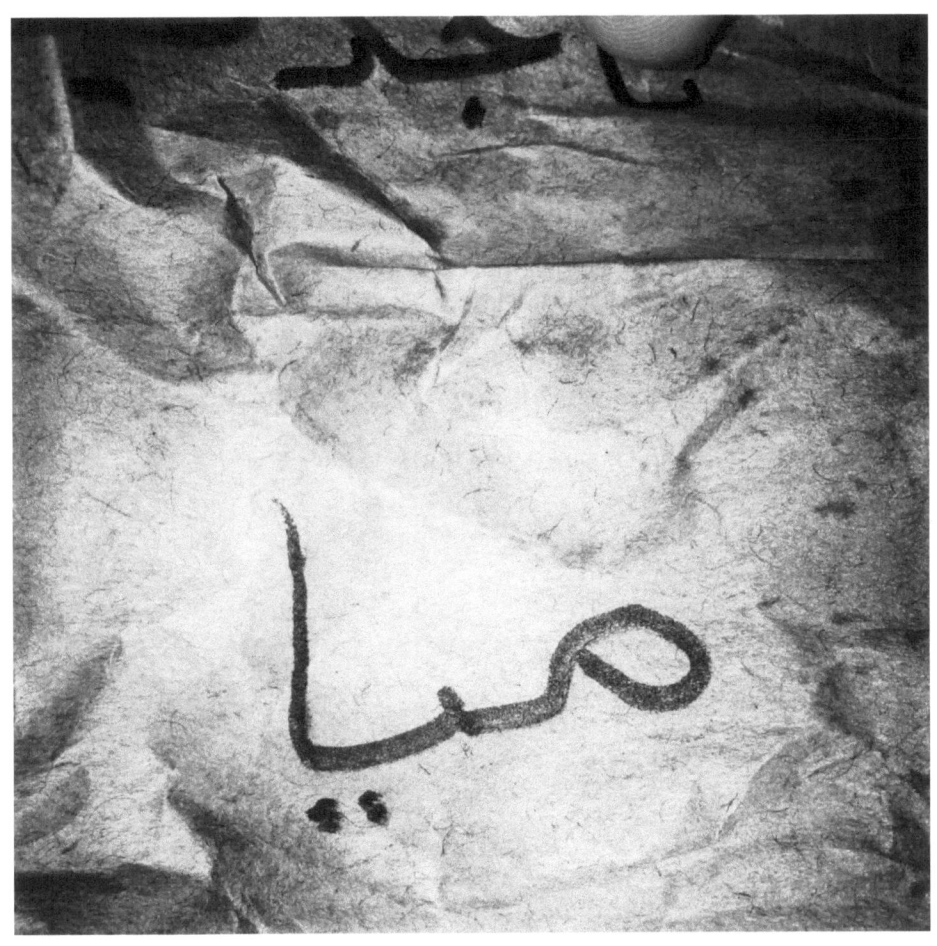

-   161st Morris avenue, BX, NY

    (Via a brown Paper bag)

Me: I need to learn Arabic, I'm tired of y'all talking about me.

Ock: You are just beautiful, what is your name.

Me: Mia, say my name so I know when you're talking about me.

Ock: This is for you, study my language.

Question: Do you believe in a higher power ?

Answer: I DON'T KNOW IF I NECESSARILY BELIEVE IN A GOD BUT I BELIEVE IN A HIGHER POWER. I GREW UP TO BELIEVE IN THIS ONE SUPREME GOD BUT I LIKE TO THINK OF GOD AS A HUGE POWER CREATED FROM SOURCES OF ENERGY. "GOD" TO ME IS A POWERFUL SOURCE THAT INFLUENCES LIVES, NOT A LITERAL MAN WHO DIED TO SAVE PEOPLE. DIFFERENT RELIGIONS HAVE THEIR NAMES FOR THEIR GOD'S BUT THEY ALL

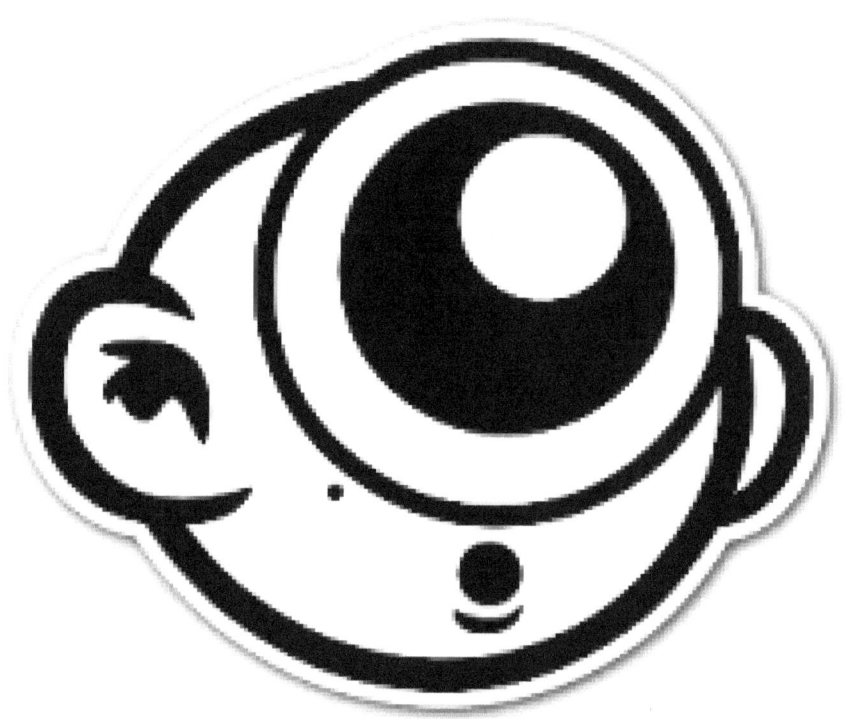

SUM UP TO THE SAME THING, A HIGHER POWER. I HAVE READ THE BIBLE, THE QURAN AND PIECES OF THE TRIPITAKA, CONCLUDING THEY ALL WERE SET OUT TO ENFORCE A CODE OF MORAL CONDUCT FOR HUMAN

BEINGS. ALTHOUGH IN DIFFERENT LANGUAGES AND SPEAKING OF DIFFERENT PEOPLE AND/OR GODS, THE BOOKS TELL A VARIETY OF STORIES, GIVEN DIFFERENT SCENARIOS, FOLLOWED BY THE OUTCOME OF THE SCENARIOS. I DO NOT CARE TO CLAIM A RELIGION, HOWEVER I DO BELIEVE IN A GOD.

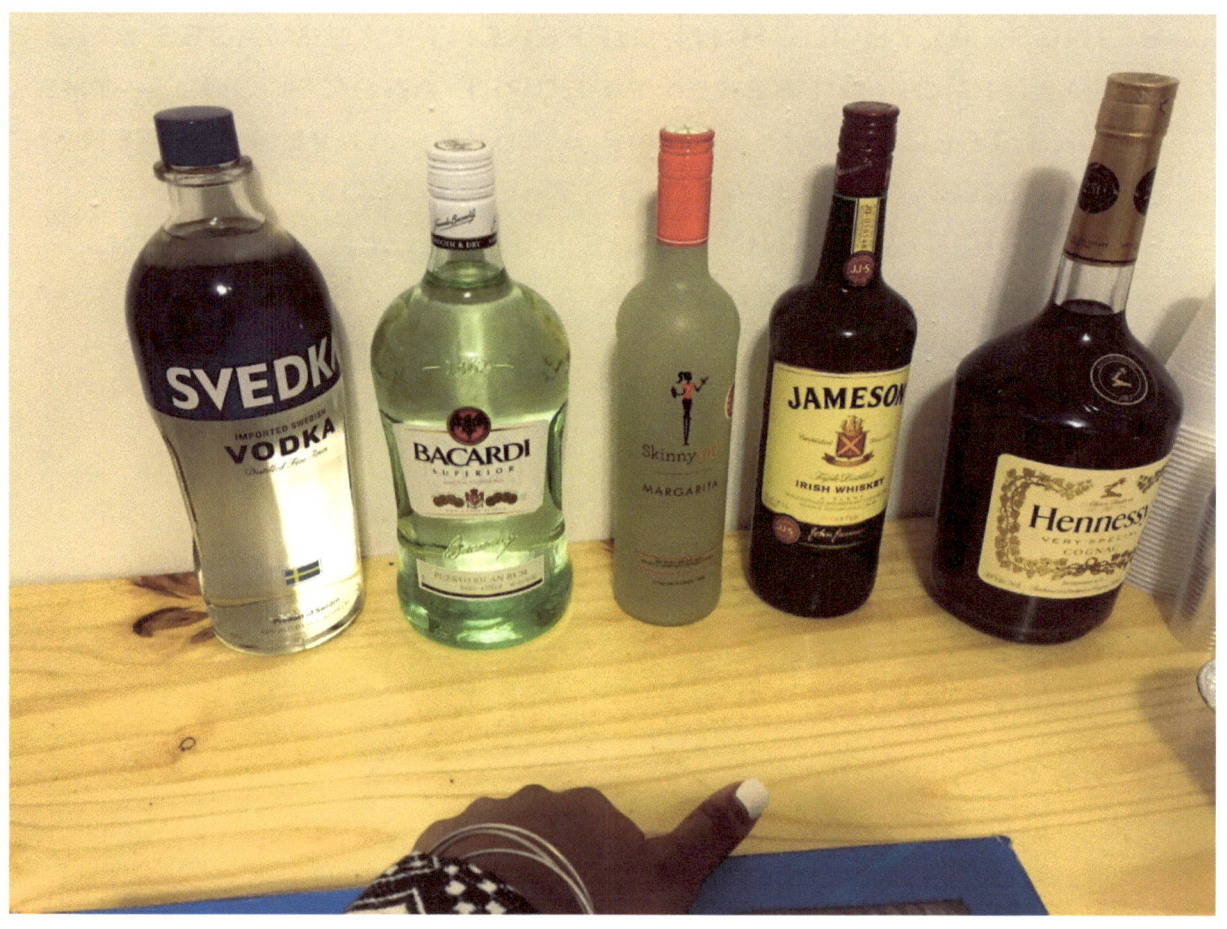

-(Some Day as a 17 year old) 198th valentine avenue, Bx, Ny

"It's only 6 Mia."

"You don't need a chaser, Mia."

"You don't have class tomorrow Mia."

"Henny thing is possible Mia."

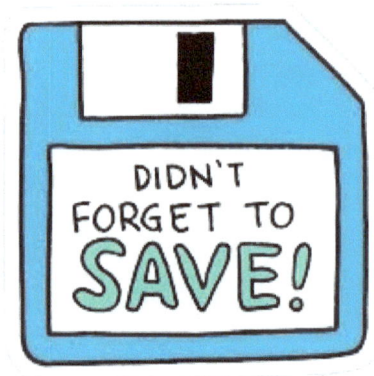

DIDN'T FORGET TO SAVE!

Mia   6/3/15

Current events

" Smart desk to keep you moving" by Jennifer Jolly (NY times)

" Smart desk to keep you moving" introduces the idea of a new smart desks that are invented to remind you to stand up every couple of hours. Studies have shown that by sitting for more than 3 hours a day cuts down your life expectancy by 2 years even if you exercise regularly. These smart desks have motion sensors that sense your movement and track your movement. They are designed to move into sitting positions and standing positions. In my opinion I think it's a stupid idea. What's the point of a chair that allows you to stand when you can just get out of the chair and stand. How does a standing chair even work , that would no longer make it a chair if you don't sit in it. However I think it is interesting that by sitting for over 3 years shortens your life expectancy by 2 years; because kids sit long hours at school and even adults sit for long periods of time when working in a office.

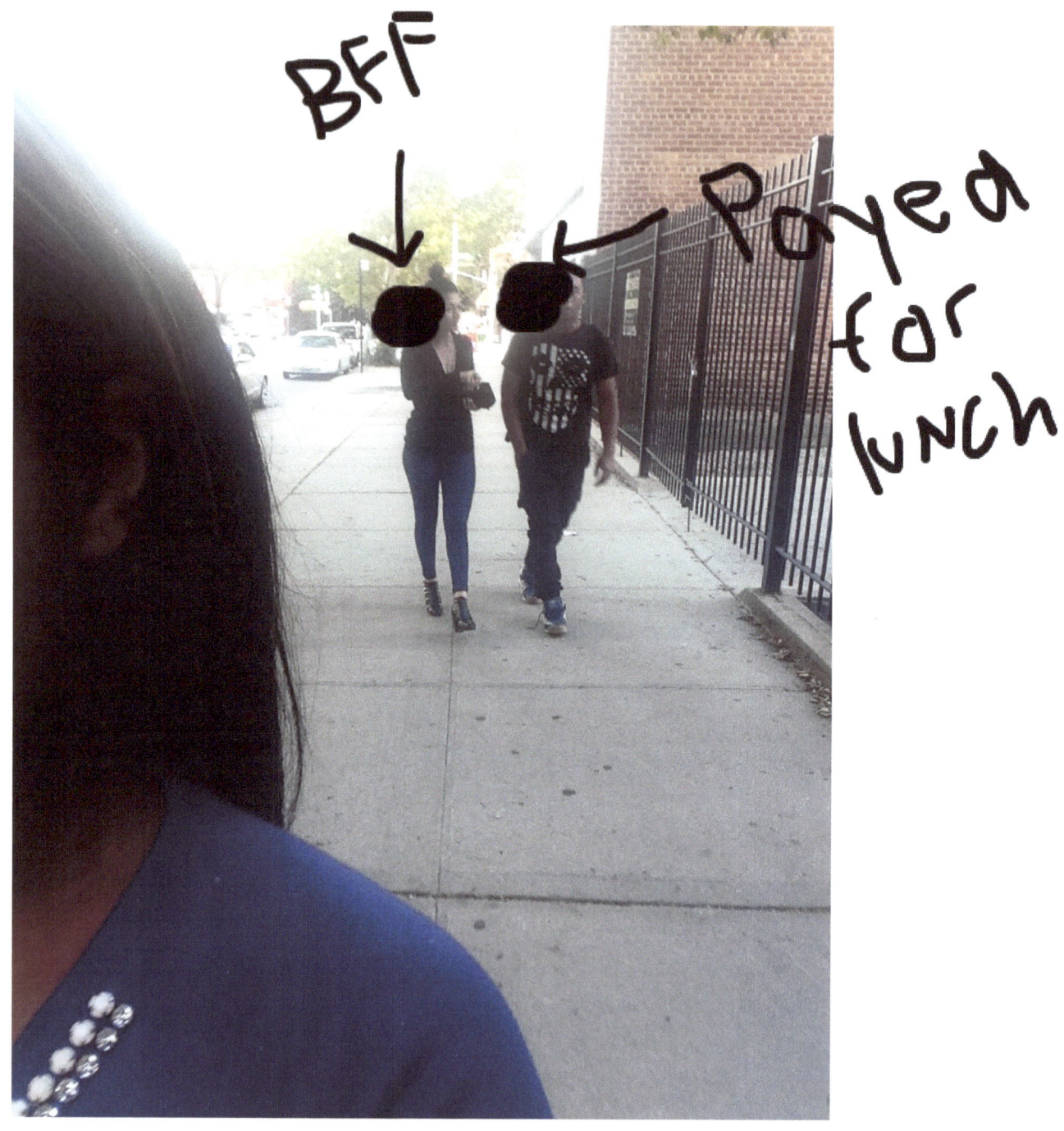

A selfie while 3rd wheeling with one of my best friends and a guy she will never speak to ever again. I just came so she didn't get kidnaped.

-Somewhere in downtown Brooklyn, 2014

Question: Should students be required to work in college?

Answer: Students shouldn't be required to work in college because its too much of a responsibility. Students have to go to class, do homework, study, eat , sleep and do normal things every other person does working is just another added on task. I understand tuition is expensive but if that's the case tuition should be lowered. Some kids might need to work in order to pay off tuition because they are not financially supported by there parents but there are always student loans. Students should have a choice if they want to work or not its there future and there money. Its bad enough students have to pay tuition having a mandatory job just makes things worst.

Are expensive prestigious private schools worth the cost ?

I think prestigious private schools are worth the cost because realistically when applying for jobs you get looked at first because your diploma is from a prestigious school. Your most likely to get a job over someone who goes to community college because you're a alumni of a ivy league or private school. Not saying that people who have degrees from private schools will be more successful In their practice due to their schools name I am just speaking realistically on how your school reflects on you.

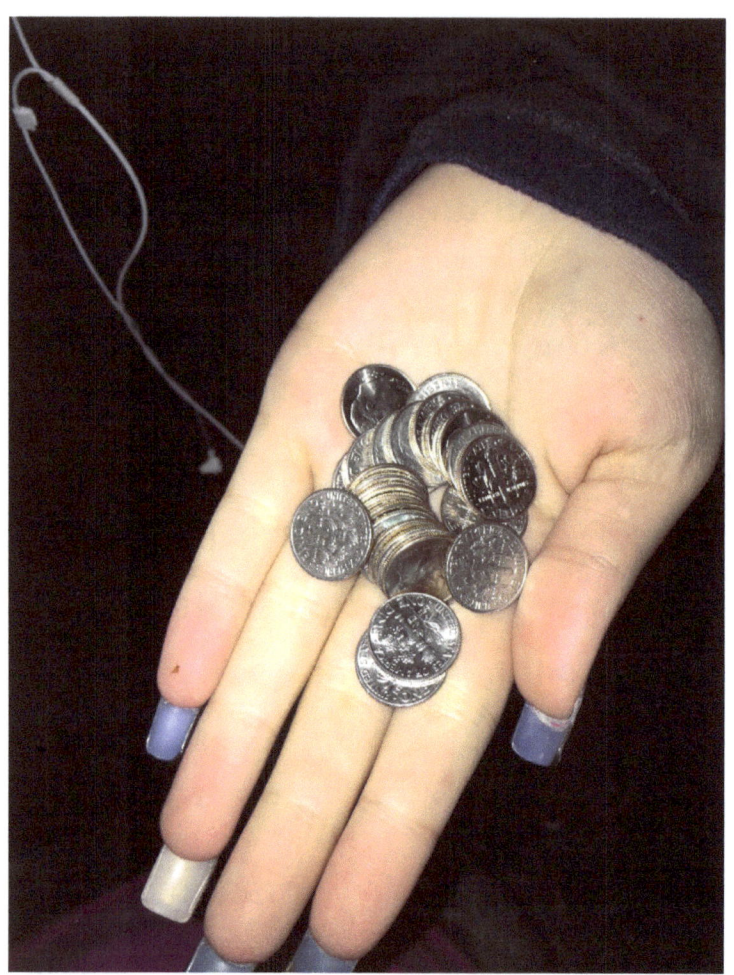

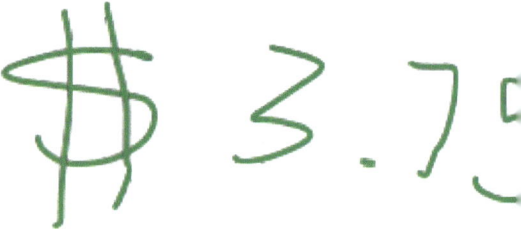

"I'm REALLY smacked and I REALLY need a chop cheese right now."

-Souly (180th street Vannest avenue, BX, NY)

A Chopped Cheese: Chopped up hamburger meat on sandwich bread. Often topped with American cheese, lettuce/tomatoes, ketchup/mayonnaise and/or onions.

- A New York City special order

- Often consumed by people under the influence of drugs

- Under the category of "Munchie food"

Mia Cruz

15 January 2016

The secret to the Secret:

The secret by Rhonda Barnes discusses how people coincide as human energy sources with the universe. The Secret also discusses the ways of the world as well as moral values that are not at all secrets; the secret is more so how to install morals and ways of thinking using energy into your everyday life.

The universe Is its own frequency which we run on. The secret compares the universes frequency to a televisions frequency. Televisions project different images on different channels which run on a frequency, we as people are made of energy and our energy works on a frequency. When you change your thoughts, you change your actions, changing your thoughts are like changing the channel of a television; a switch in frequency causes a switch in the picture. Therefore a switch in your energy causes a switch in the picture (the television show) , the picture or episode being your life.

A major issue discussed is the "Don't epidemic". The don't epidemic is how people unknowingly send out bad energy and attract negative things to them. One of the main points in this book is the law of attraction. People are like magnets and the things you think about is what will come to you. A magnet picks up another magnet because they both have the same properties so they attract one another, we may not understand exactly how it works but that's just how it is. In this book it is emphasized how important it is to be positive because what you put out into the universe is what you will get back. When you use words like "Don't" and "Can't" you are sending out negative energy even if they are used in a positive way. For example in English when a word has a negative connotation and it is used in a sentence the whole sentence automatically has a negative connotation. This law is common sense people are just unaware of how to keep their energy leveled on a daily basis.

Aladdin and the genie are used to explain the law of attraction and how it has been acknowledged over the years and put into a children's story to install this thinking process in your mind at a early age. Aladdin was a poor boy who meets a genie, the genie grants aladdin 3 wishes and tells him there are no limitations on what he may wish for. Genie moves, changes and manipulates the world around him to grant aladdin these wishes. Aladdin is you, The Genie is the universe and his wishes are your thoughts. By sending out your wishes through your thoughts the world will pick up these thoughts and change itself in order to align everyone to the frequencies they are shifting towards. At the end of the story aladdin meets a princess and falls in love, you may be asking how does that relate to the law of attraction.

Love is believed to be one of the highest frequencies and that was the most empowering lessons I have learned in this whole book. Love Doesn't necessarily mean relationship wise, you can never truly love if you don't love yourself. The reason people say to be grateful for the life you live is because those people understand the concept of love so they are content with what they have even if they only have themselves. When you love yourself you don't focus all your energy into finding love so your then able to send out all of your positive energy into the universe!

27

Oni: Mia I'm hungry, come on so we can meet nana!!!

Me: Just take a picture of me and bae!!

Oni: Mia no!

6 minutes later

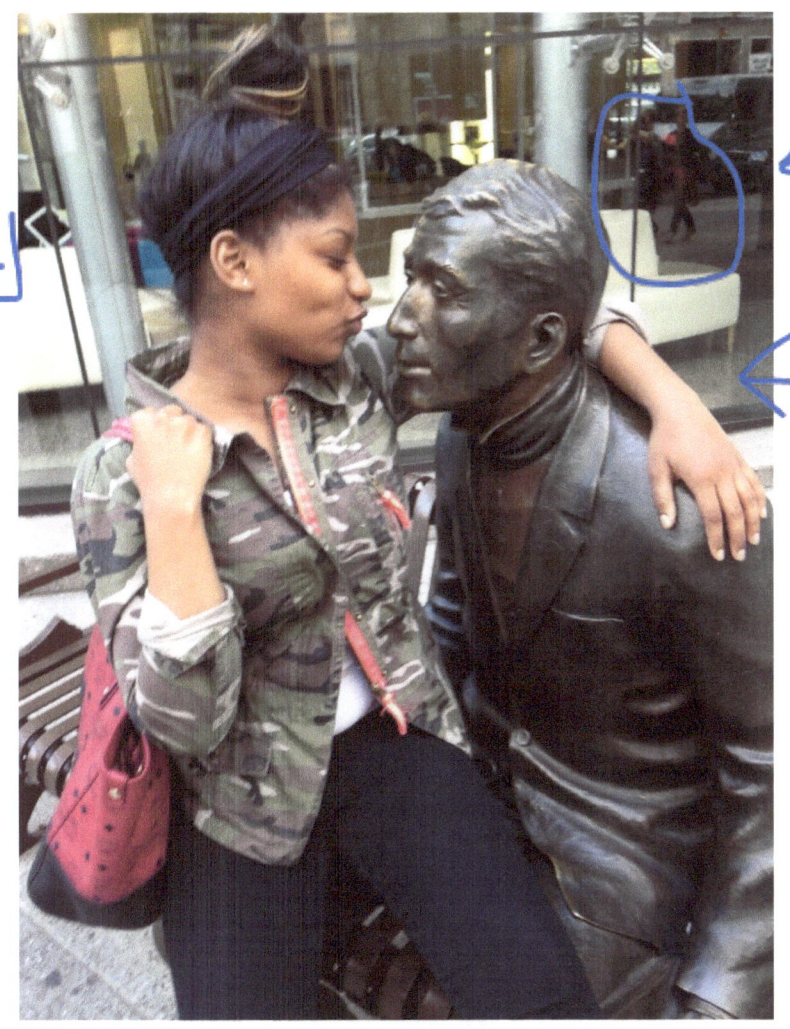

-(A Tuesday in 2014) west 61st street and Broadway ave, NY, NY

Mia Cruz

17 November 2015

Guilt by Default

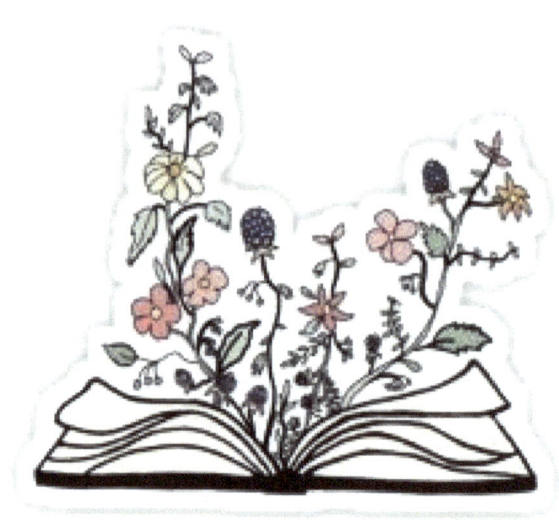

THE CRUCIBLE WAS BASED ON A TIME IN HISTORY WHERE GUILT AND INNOCENCE WAS INFLUENCED BY FEAR AND NOT BASED OFF OF FACTUAL EVIDENCE. THE CRUCIBLE ILLUSTRATED THE INJUSTICES OF SALEM'S THEOCRACY AND HOW THIS EVENT INFLUENCED THE LIVES OF NOT ONLY THE VICTIMS BUT OF A WHOLE TOWN. THROUGHOUT THE STORY THERE ARE CHARACTERS WHO WRONGFULLY ACCUSE OTHERS AS WELL AS CHARACTERS WHO CONFESS TO FALSE ACCUSATIONS OUT OF FEAR.

THERE WAS A SPIRAL EFFECT THAT LED TO THE DEATHS OF MANY PEOPLE THROUGHOUT THE PLAY, ALL STARTING WITH JOHN PROCTOR HAVING AN AFFAIR WITH ABIGAIL WILLIAMS. IN THE BEGINNING OF THE PLAY RUTH PUTNAM SENT HER DAUGHTER OUT TO THE WOODS WITH THE SLAVE TITUBA TO PRACTICE WITCHCRAFT TO FIND OUT WHY 7 OF HER CHILDREN DIED AT BIRTH; ABIGAIL AND OTHER GIRLS FROM THE TOWN JOINED RUTH. ABIGAIL'S UNCLE, REVEREND

Parris spotted the girls dancing and singing while running naked in the woods. Once Abigail was confronted she claimed she seen John Proctor's wife, Elizabeth Proctor with the devil. Abigail Accused Elizabeth of Witchcraft not because she was guilty but because she had hopes of being with John. Early on in the play Abigail and Betty got into a argument, "You drank a charm to kill John Proctors wife! You drank a charm to kill Goody Proctor!" (19) said Ruth to Abigail implying she knows Abigail's true intentions towards Elizabeth.

Theocracy was one of the main factors that led to the hangings of the people in the crucible. In act one after Abigail was confronted about being in the woods with the other girls, Betty Paris pretended to lay ill due to witchcraft. Once the town becomes aware the court became involved: inviting a Respected Reverend named Hale to help the investigation. later on in the play Hale comes to a realization that the way these people are being prosecuted is not fair or based on evidence. Hales purpose in Salem was to help find witches and as the story progressed, so did his thoughts on Salem's theocracy. In act 4 when John Proctor Was offered to keep his life in return for a confession, Hale pleaded with John Proctor telling his wife " Let him give his lie. Quail not before God's judgment in this, for it may well be God damns a liar less than he that throws his life away for pride" (132). At this point Hale is starting to realize how fear has an effect over the people of Salem.

Judge Danforth, a judge of high authority in Salem who handled the trials also was a character whose views changed as the play progressed. He carried out the trials based off of nothing but allegations and accusations most of which were not correct.In the beginning of the play Danforth's tactics where to guilt people into confessing to witchcraft because he truly believed they were witches. In the last act of the play when John Proctor was soon to be hung,

DANFORTH REALIZES HIS FAULTS. DANFORTH PLEADES TO ELIZABETH TELLING HER "BE THERE NO WIFELY TENDERNESS WITHIN YOU? HE WILL DIE WITHIN THE SUNRISE … WILL YOU CONTEND WITH HIM?" (132). AT THIS POINT IN THE PLAY DANFORTH IS NOW PLEADING WITH JOHN PROCTOR TO CONFESS NOT BECAUSE HE IS TRULY GUILTY BUT OUT OF FEAR PEOPLE WILL REALIZE HIS WRONG JUDGMENT THAT HAS RESULTED IN THE DEATH OF INNOCENT PEOPLE.

31

Mia Cruz

28, September, 2016

(The Learning experience co.)

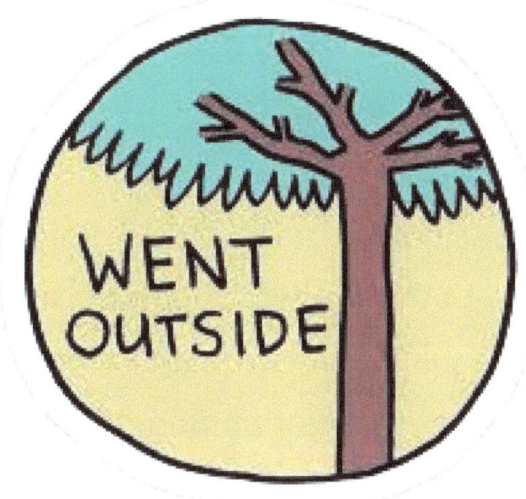

The Learning experience is a corporation that offers early education programs run across the country. The learning experience started in 1980 which was co-founded by Mr. Michael Weismann and Ms. Linda Weisman, originating as 1 location in Boca Raton, FL, run by the Weismann Family. This program is now available in 16 states (New Jersey, New York, Pennsylvania, Michigan, North Carolina, Connecticut, Illinois, Georgia, Massachusetts, New Hampshire, Minnesota, Texas, Arizona, Colorado, Florida, and Virginia);

providing service for Toddlers, Preschoolers, Pre kindergarteners, as well as after care for children up to eight years' old.

I chose this particular business to research because not only have I been seeing the company more often I am also very interested in the way our education system works in all aspects. The learning experience is available in over 15 states, meaning in 15 states there are thousands of children who are prepped for school through this program, that is significant considering it is not government run. I appreciate the hard work and dedication people give towards bettering the education of children who are not even their own, in my opinion teaching is not an easy task so I find it honorable; education is not granted to everyone, let alone the ability of being able to teach others. I applaud all those who spend any amount of time towards bettering other people, especially children considering we are truly the future.

I believe This business will be and already is very successful. Education is something that will always be necessary, teachers will always be needed, not all parents work from home or at all and are able to watch their children, and due to these factors I cannot think of one reason as to why this business will not succeed or proceed to expand in the future. The learning experience's over all business reports are exceptional and many people have given positive feedback in regards to their academic programs as well as the care of their children.

This would be a Business and industry I would be interested in but not to work, to invest. I know I personally do not have the patience to teach especially with children, I am more of the art teacher to let a single class use all of our water color paint for the month. However, I would always be interested in investing money into education whether it be children, adults, disabled, special needs; Education is very important to me. I might not necessarily agree with Every education system or programs however the idea in itself, to education others give me gratification. This a business that started from one location and expanded to over 15 states, statistically proving they are running not only an exceptional education program but a beneficial program that is able to be adjusted as needed. Due to the fact it isn't a department of education program is also another big factor as to why I would be interested, I love the fact average people started to create something so beneficial solely to give something as important as education to their local community; 30 years later they have succeeded far beyond 1 little location in Boca Raton, Fl.

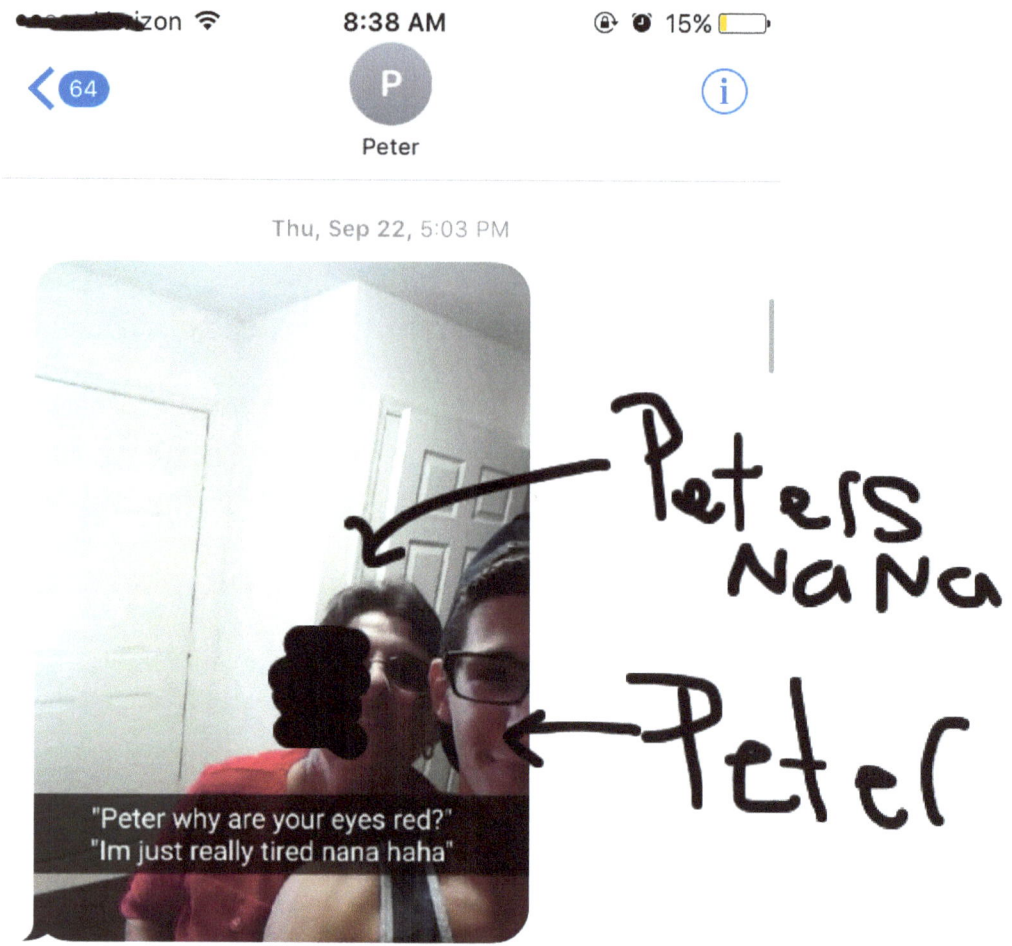

Cyph definition: When a group of two or more people get high together.

Example: Peter has weed and Q has a wrap, therefore peter sent q a text asking if he wants to Cyph.

10/8/15

How To Spot a Witch:

Purpose behind Witchcraft: Witches practice their craft to help create balance in the world. Portions were created to soothe the mentals and bring comfort to those in need of help.Practicing Witchcraft is not about immediate physical changes but about the mental state they can take themselves to as well as the people around them. By allowing yourself to be frightened of witches your not allowing ourself to be introduced to their energy. With feelings come actions, with Actions come change, with mental awakening comes physical reactions.

Spirit marks and Energy stamps: physical marks do not define a witch, there spiritual marks do. Freckles, moles, dimples, and pigmentation are nothing but marks used to distract you from the actual marks that you should pay attention to. Good witches have marks that can only be seen through conversation. For years witches have stayed hidden not because they are keeping dangerous secrets but to protect themselves. They stay hidden to keep their energy levels positive. You will never fully switch your energy level to that of a witch until you seek It out.

Witches testing society: Witches are healers however they are not responsible for saving the world. Staying hidden away is a witches way of testing society. If witches went out into the world trying to radiate positive energy they could fall into the evil ways of society and change energy levels.Those who need help or want to live happy lives will go seek fulfillment with in this positive energy. Although hidden they can be found when called upon by your spirits. The same way people fall in love and can feel chemistry is the same way you and a witch can pick up on one another's energy; even when our unaware of it.

Asking the right questions: "the right questions" will not let you know if someone is a witch but what kind of witch they are. Like everything els in the world there is both good and bad. Being a good witch comes with the responsibility of protecting, securing & being optimistic."The right questions" are questions that will allow you to see into the spirit of a witch. How far are they willing to go to make you spiritually aware ? How much effort are they willing to put in to help you overcome or reduce any negative energy you come in contact with?

What can the do to help soothe you in times of discomfort or unfortunate circumstances ? Don't let one bad witch stop you from seeking out your inner witch.

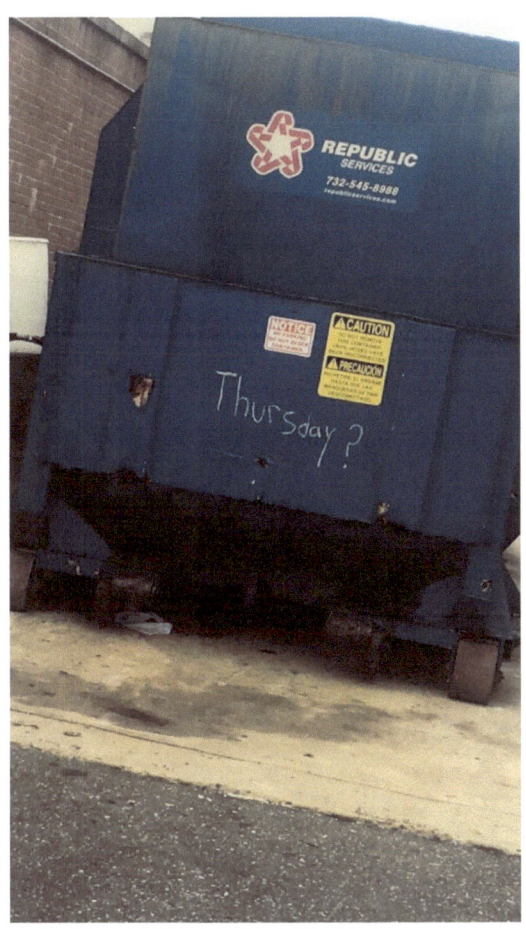

Friday 10/21/16 :

- Marine bio: Worksheet

- English: Grendal questions

Thursday 10/25/16:

?

?

?

19 March 2014

The great gatsby does not represent the American I live in. The great Gatsby is a commercialized vision of America, created to present America as a creative place where all have the opportunity to create great lives for themselves which is not the case. It's the ideal time era to live in because of their strong values that have been lost in modern day America.

In The Great gatsby film the people's value's seemed to be very materialistic and they value status. Gatsby and Tom, two of the main male characters are men of high authority due to their economic statuses. People cater to them and show respect because they know they are rich men and at this time not many people where, they would somewhat be modern day celebrities. However the people in this time also valued the company of others. Gatsby's parties where filled regularly with Random people who came just to have a good time regardless of economic status; parties where thrown regularly where people simply danced and listened to music not to network but for fun. Having tea was a casual occasion just to enjoy the company of others, today people think coming together and enjoying each others company should only be done on special occasions.

This film is more About America in the 1920's before technology had such an effect on everyday life. In the film they emphasize how much fun people had carefree. This movie shows how life for these people changed everyday because there was not much structure socially or government wise. Gatsby acquired his wealth by selling and transporting liquor which was illegal at the time, everyone of the time was aware of gatsby's wealth but not of how he earned it. Today that could never really happen in America because our government would quickly become aware of the illegal affairs due to the fact he was a well known man who also lived locally in one the most popular states in the country. Today majority of the money circulated is tracked and monitored, all traces of unaccounted money would raise red flags and Gatsby wouldn't have come far up the ladder of success.

In this film the great gatsby Luhrmann made every scene so animated that he didn't emphasize the actual life of middle class/ poor people living in this time. Everything was made to look like it was a celebration, however this showed the importance of their values. There were no low points in the movie that displayed what living was really like for people who were not rich, everything seemed to be glitter and gold which is not how America was in the 1920s or today. Therefore I don't think this film displays my contemporary culture. In my culture the same values in the great Gatsby are not present, people today are more consumed with self accomplishments and less about enjoying life with the company of others. Today celebrities are appraised for having reached an amount of followers on social media or for slandering others online Not for extending their wealth with others or being nice people like Gatsby was. Celebrities today would fall more under the category of Tom Bucanon who use their wealth only to the benefit of themselves.

This film did a good job of adapting the novel yet not a good enough job. The film was exciting and graphic, making the storyline and time period seem very ideal. The film was contradictory of the book because of the character who told the story. The Main character Nick Carraway (the cousin of Daisy Buchanan) was the narrator of the story and because of this it calls into question how accurate or even misleading the relationship between Gatsby and Daisy was. If Nick was the narrator how was he able to know what happened privately between gatsby and daisy, which changes everything because although Nick was also the narrator in the book there was less vivid details on the romance of Gatsby and Daisy. The book, because Told from Nicks point of view emphasized the hope and promise of gatsby having a relationship with daisy versus the movie which focused on the actual relationship they had. However the film did an exceptional job at Showing how extravagant Gatsby's parties where and how involved the people of the era where in enjoying themselves.

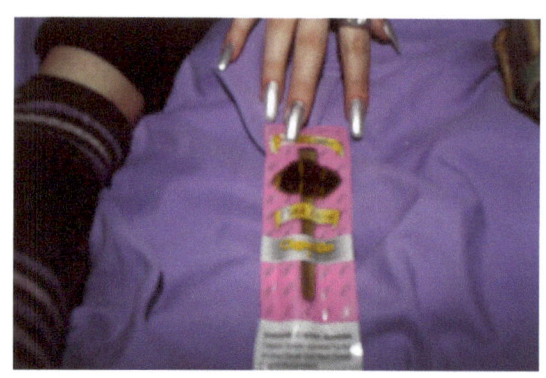

Prefrontal lobe is effected the most when under the

THC

(psychosomati

CBD

(Medical

Cannab

Doesn't kill

Wee

Cannot kill you, unless you Smoke the equivalence of

Naturally 80 unites

Dopami

Coffee – 100 unites

Neurotransmitters

Indic

Sativ

Marijuana-150

moo

Shorter and

Tall and Thin

Cocaine – 300

Dark

Light

Crystal Meth – 1500

*CBD relaxes nerve impulses to

Pain

Upliftin

Fluff

Cerebr

Sedativ

19 September 2016

Donald Trump's Fallacy reasonings

Donald Trump's foreign policy consisted of many fallacies such as Post hoc ergo propter hoc, Ad hominem and Ad populum. I strongly believe majority if not all of his Campaign tactics consist of multiple fallacies; He Constantly attacks and bombards people as well as their thoughts and beliefs to try and validate his absurd arguments.

Mid August of 2016 Trump gave his foreign policy speech; it was full of lies and discredited our current president Obama as well as current runner for the 2016 election, Hillary Clinton. He tries to use ad hominem to persuade his audience by making accusations about Us relations that insinuate we have been put in danger unconsciously by current president Barack Obama. Ad hominem is a fallacy that attacks the character of a person instead of the actual issue. Trump quotes " we're in a war against radical Islam, but president Obama won't even name the enemy!" in referral to Obama's refusal to call Terrorist, such as isis "Islamic extremist" , when Obama has clarified many times that he will not single out a single religion for the sake of the publics peace of mind. Trump is attempting to discredit Obama's name as well as negatively associate the people of the Islamic religion.

Trump continues to Attack the Islamic people in his speech using Ad populum fallacy which is when you try to emotionally suede a argument positivly or in this case negatively. He continues to victimize Christians by saying " We left Christians subject to intense persecution and even genocide." Trump is now referring to the Butchering of Christians in Iraq and using it to push the idea of all Islamic people being terrorist. Not only is this a fallacy because its untrue but because he clearly did not care to do his research. Majority of Isis's victims have been Muslim victims not Christians; He is attempting to Appeal to Christian voters as well as Cause more negative association with the religion of Islam and followers of the religion.

While reading Trumps speech in further detail a rather big fallacy I came across was his belief in rebuilding Americas relationships with other countries. Trump uses ad hominem fallacy to talks about Obama's written agreement with Iraq regarding their use of missiles and how it blatantly was disregarded by Iraq. However there has been no proof that missiles have been launched in Iraq besides reported missile testing. He later goes on to say How America is not traveling abroad to create enemies but rather friends; yet he constantly contradicts himself by talking down on many terms and agreements made with other countries to create peace, including obamas deal with Iraq. He uses ad hominem fallacy constantly when beneficial to his argument instead of clearly addressing problems and creating solutions.

Donald Trumps Speech on foreign policy had multiple arguments that where both insensitive and contradictory to many of his arguments made prior to this speech. Therefore His speech perfectly displayed the many ways in which you can create fallacy reasoning.

20 word about your first job:

Want to start by saying I hate you all. Between rude and stupid
people, I quit.

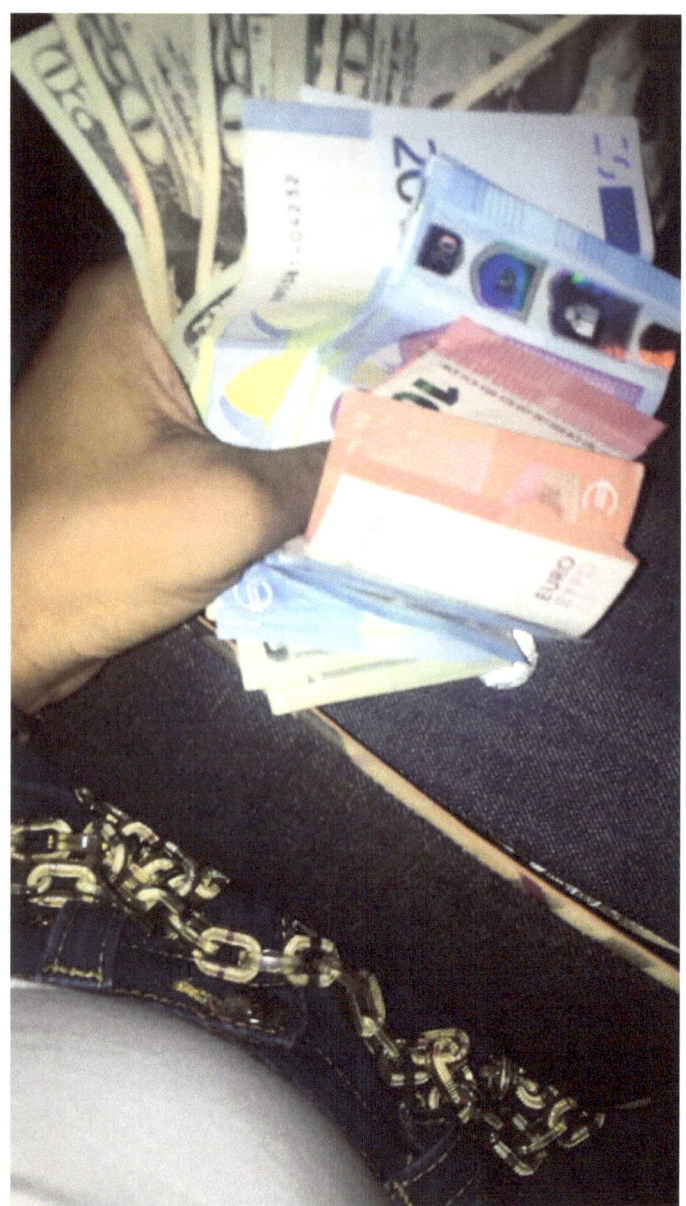

<u>3 stupid commonly asked questions in the food customer service world:</u>

- **Q:** How long has that been out?

  Answer we give you: about 15 minutes.

  The answer we wish we could give you: 4 hours, but I'm still gonna put it in a bowl and serve it with a spoon because that's my job.

- **Q:** Which coffee pot is the freshest?

  Answer we give you: These are all freshly brewed.

  The answer we wish we could give you: we don't keep track of coffee pots, I don't get paid for that.

- **Q:** Are these on sale?

  Answer we give you: Sorry no, it doesn't ring up on sale.

  The answer we wish we could give you: Just because you ask me if its on sale doesn't mean I am going to mark it on sale, nice try though.

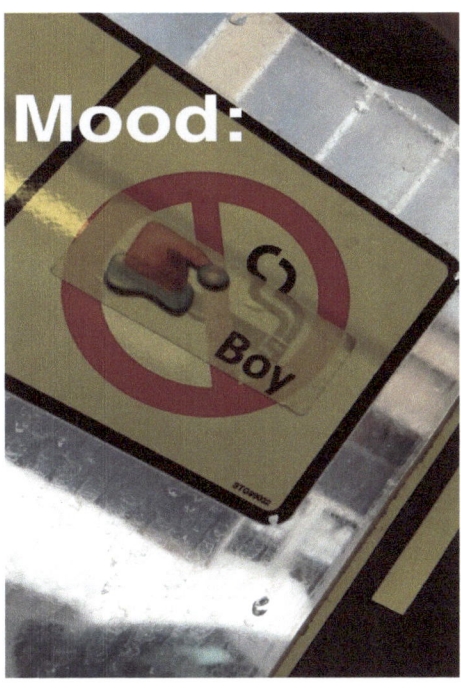

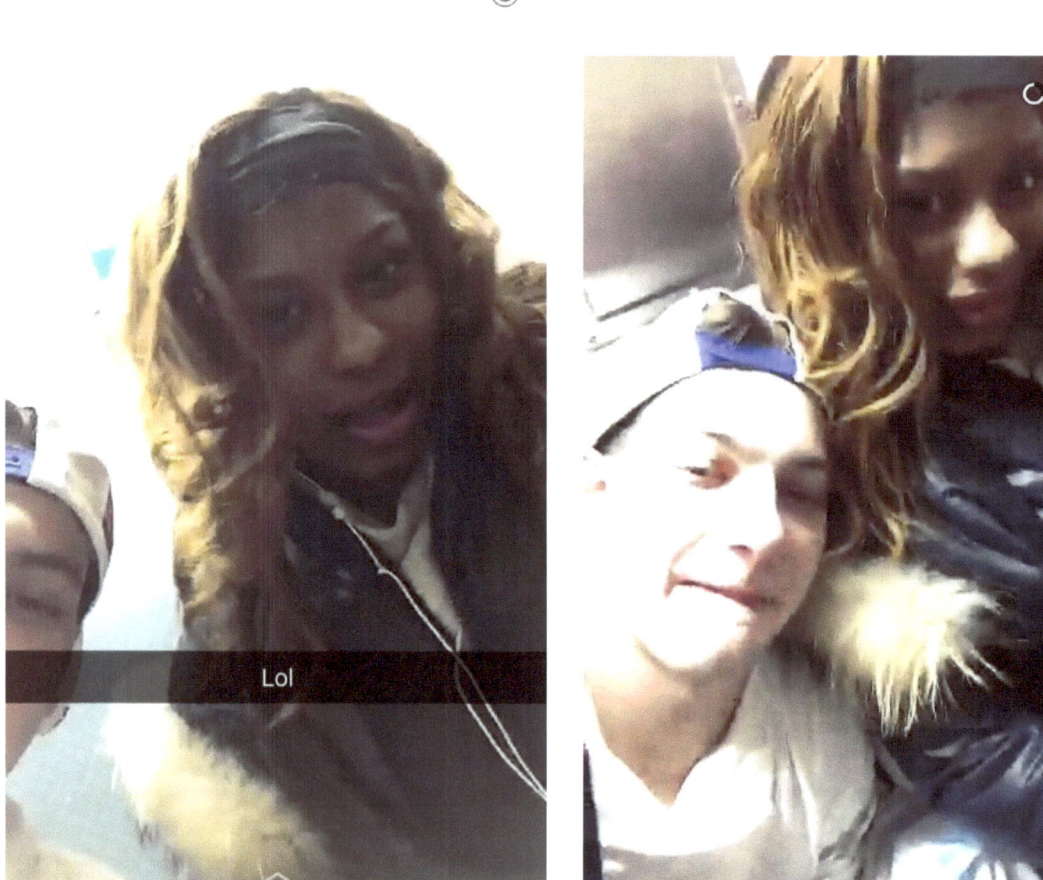

Me: *um excuse you, you're leaning on me.*

Random guy Mike: *I'm drunk and I have no money. Your really cute, can I put you on my snap.*

Me: *I don't know you, but hi snap.*

<u>3 Easy steps to get rid of all the basic bitches in your life:</u>

Step 1. Gather

Step 2. Analyze

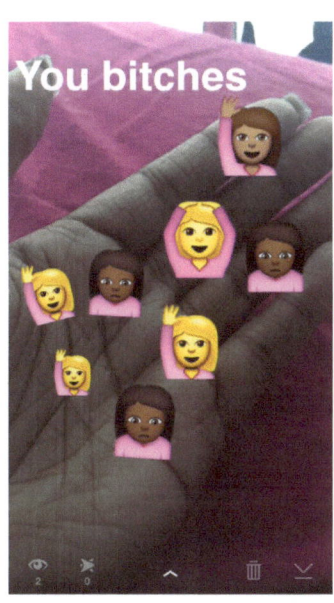

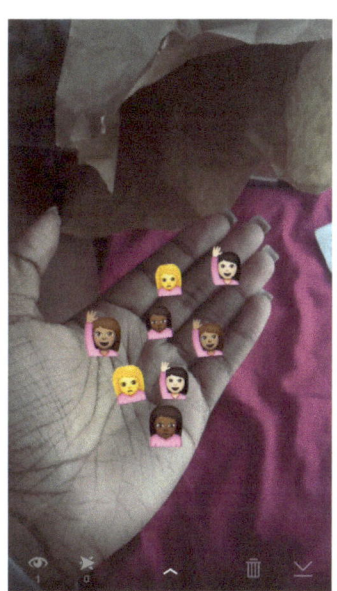

Step 3. Dispose of them.

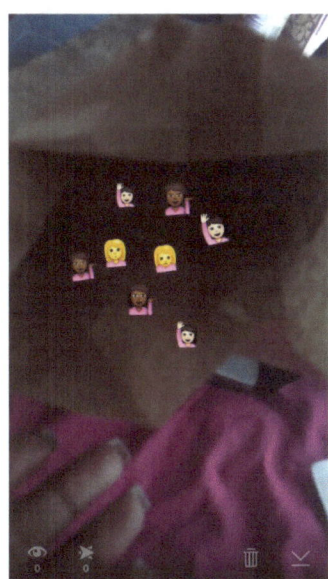

Q: What was it like going to a Primarily White school being Hispanic?

A: IT WAS HORRIBLE CONSIDERING HOW IGNORANT PEOPLE ARE. ATTENDING SCHOOL IN OLDBRIDGE, NEW JERSEY WAS LIKE SOMETHING OUT OF A MOVIE. MANY STUDENTS AND TEACHERS ARE IN DESPERATE NEED OF DIVERSITY AND CULTURAL AWARENESS. IF YOUR SKIN COLOR IS ANYTHING DARKER THAN YELLOW, YOU ARE PLACED IN A DIFFERENT CATEGORY AND LOOKED AT DIFFERENTLY. I HAVE BEEN ASKED SO MANY IGNORANT QUESTIONS AND HEARD SO MANY RACIAL, DISCRIMINATIVE COMMENTS; BUT NEVER MORE THAN I HAVE WHILE ATTENDING SCHOOL IN NEW JERSEY. COMMENTS ABOUT NOT BEING HISPANIC BECAUSE MY SKIN IS TOO "BLACK," NOT BEING INVITED TO THE BEACH BECAUSE APPARENTLY I " DON'T NEED ANYMORE SUN,," I HAVE WALKED DOWN THE HALLS AND HEARD CAUCASIAN'S CALLING EACH OTHER "MY NIGGA" WITH NO HESITATION, SEEN AFRICAN AMERICAN KIDS CURSE OUT THERE PARENTS BECAUSE THEY COULDN'T AFFORD TO GIVE THEM THE SAME THINGS THERE RICH CAUCASIAN FRIENDS WERE GIVEN. BEFORE I CONTINUE I WANT TO SAY I AM NOT OPPOSED TO PEOPLE EXPRESSING THEMSELVES OR DISPLAYING TRENDS PROMINENTLY DISPLAYED BY RACES OTHER THAN YOUR OWN; HOWEVER I AM OPPOSED TO CULTURAL DIVERSITY IN EFFECT FOR THE WRONG REASONS. I SEE KIDS WHO ARE FILLED WITH SELF HATE AND GO BEYOND MEASURES TO CHANGE THEMSELVES IN ORDER TO FIT IN

WITH THE PEOPLE AROUND THEM. AFRICAN AMERICAN KIDS WITH BEACH BLOND HAIR, HAZEL CONTACTS, BROKEN SIZZLED HAIR FROM FLAT IRONING EVERY DAY WALK THE HALLS PROUDLY BECAUSE THEY FEEL LIKE THEY "FIT IT". CAUCASIAN KIDS WALK DOWN THE HALL WEARING "WAVES" IN THEIR HAIR THEN MAKE FUN OF THE AFRICAN AMERICAN KID WHO HAS THE SAME HAIRSTYLE BECAUSE HIS SKIN COLOR IS DARKER. IT DISGUSTS ME THAT IT IS 2017 AND I HAVE CLASSMATES WHO HAVE OPENLY RACIST PARENTS AND PEERS WHO WILL NOT INVITE THEIR FRIENDS WHO DON'T HAVE BLOND HAIR OR WHITE SKIN BECAUSE THEIR PARENTS WON'T ALLOW THEM INTO THEIR HOMES.

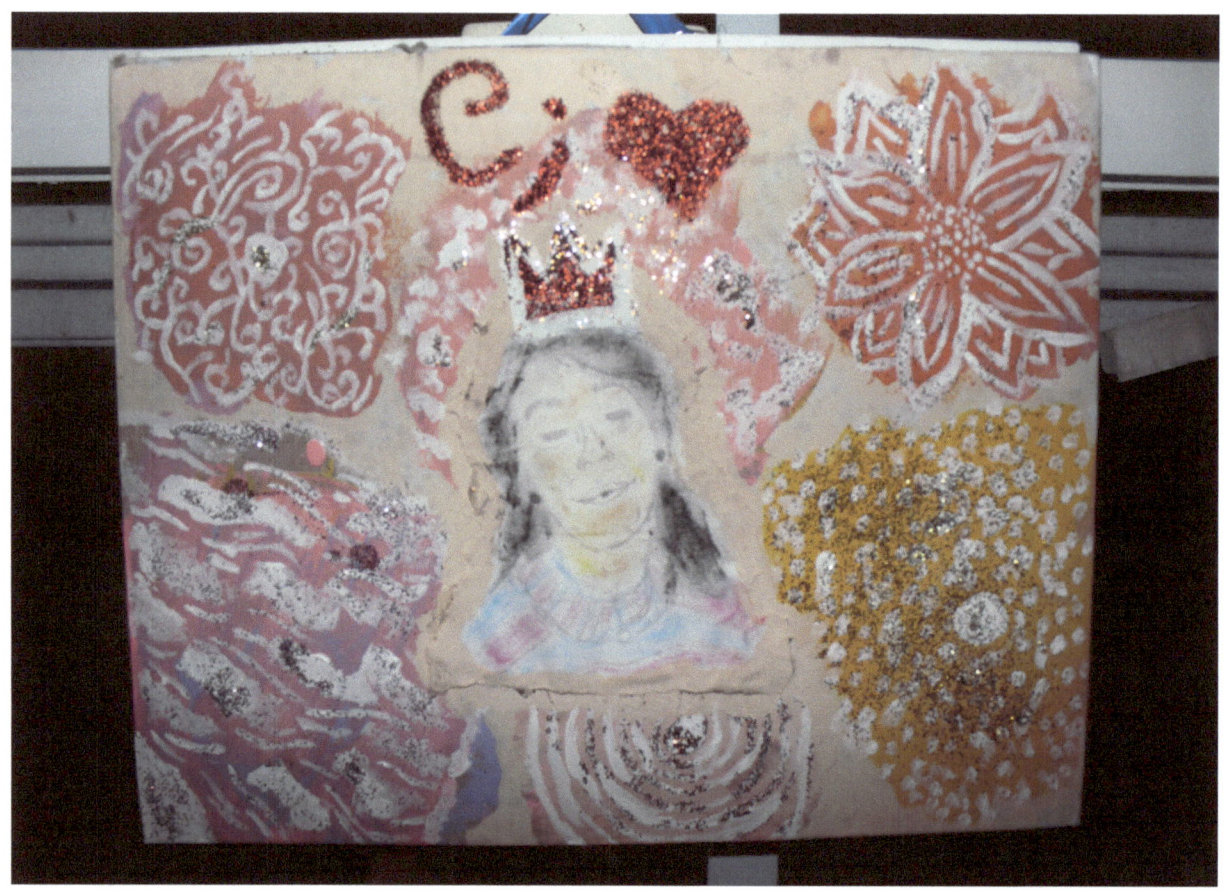

Title: *Strawberry field*

Artist: *Mia Moore*

Year: *2016*

" Once upon a time there was a princess named Carmacita..." - The Real Puertorican Princess

8, January, 2017

The wrath of achilies has been felt and expressed for centuries, it's influence forever a part of history. This resulted in one of the best literary works today; The Iliad. The famous Achilles, a well known Greek war hero, had strengths beyond measure (partial to the fact he was a Demi god) along with great influence and authority over the Greek army. Achilles prideful disposition created a domino effect ending the lives of many and eventually his own. Homer used Achilles authority on the people of Greece to emphasize the influence he had on the fait of the people and how it ultimately led to his own.

Achilles wrath originated out of his hate for the leader of the Greek army, Agamemnon who was envious of Achilles because he couldn't compare to Achilles in battle. Agamemnon took the daughter of a priest and refused to return her, once the father became aware of this he prayed for the downfall of the Greek army and the god Phoebus heard him. In response the priest " shot fiery arrows down upon the Greek army.." (Iliad 263) He seeked out revenge on Agamemnon by sickening and killing the soldiers so much so " the funeral pyres were burning continuously."(Iliad 263) Achilles went in search of answers by holding an uncalled meeting discovering Agamemnon's selfish choice was the reason behind the defeat of the Greek army. Achilles refused to fight or advise the Greek army while under the control of Agamemnon. Knowing that Agamemnon had no chance of fighting without Achilles, the fait of the Greek people changes instantly.

Achilles decides to leave the lives of the Greek soldiers and civilians in the balance because of his motive to seek revenge on Agamemnon. During the Trojans attack on the Greeks, he was faced with the choice to fight or hold out on battle refusing to give Agamemnon the satisfaction. During this battle Patroclus, Achilles close friend encourages him to fight and in response Achilles affirms he will not fight, quoting " For my own ships, If the battle comes near them, I will fight. I will not fight for men who have disgraced me." (Iliad 271) In this part of the story the two switch armors in attempt to throw off the Trojan soldiers, Achilles well aware of the sacrifice he would be making to have his friends life taken instead of his own. I believe homer used this scene to talk about life and death on a personal level to emphasize how far Achilles was willing to go in honor of his revenge against Agamemnon.

Prior to achilles death he receives warning multiple times; sea nymph Thetis, the mother of Achilles, warned him " To have nothing more to do with the Greeks... And asked Zues to give success to the trojans." (Iliad 264) During the Trojan war Achilles ultimately faces his death by being shot in his Achilles heel, although not mentioned directly in the Iliad. His wrath determined history, if not for his rage he would not have left the lives of thousands up to chance in refusal to fight alongside Agamemnon including his own. Achilles was a honorable soldier who was known for his fighting skills and abilities; however every action he made out of anger lead to his own death.

If not for Achilles rage the Greek possibly could have succeeded in taking over the Trojans prior to the Trojan war. If not for his need to seek revenge he wouldn't have lost his life or had to sacrifice the lives of his loved ones. Although he didn't lose his life fighting in battle as he planned he still lost his life because of events that he influenced and had control over. He could have listened to his mother and dropped his association with the Greeks all together but he didn't out of pride and honor. The selfish choices made of out rage is what fueled such a tragic ending for such a famous Greek war hero.

Q: What is your favorite physical feature?

A:

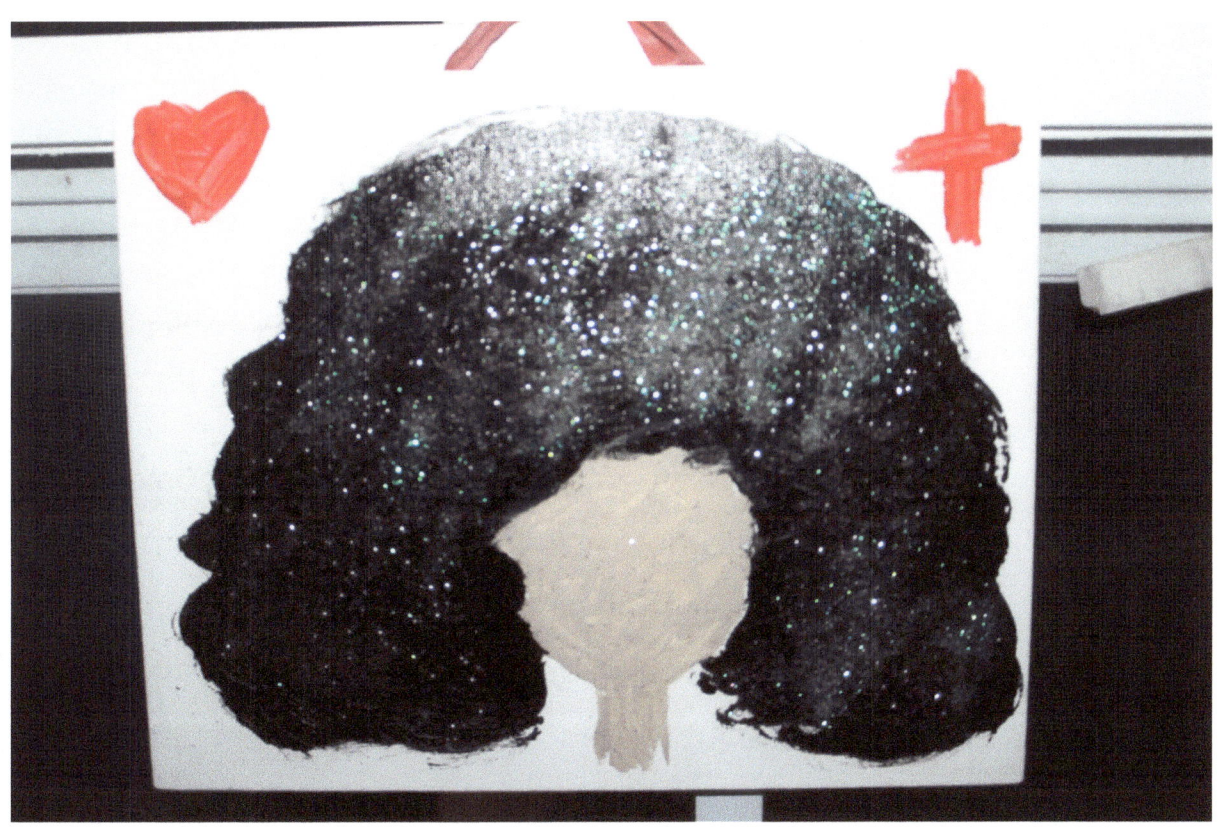

Title: Monica Marie

Artist: Mia Moore

Year: 2017

07, March, 2015

World Wide Tec Support

The world we live in is consumed with and ran by technology. Headlines often introduce technology as advances in todays society but don't necessarily explain the pros and cons it will have on our future. These new inventions may be convenient and have positive impacts however they have negative impacts on people as well. Why should one listen to society promote these new Technological advances with out knowing the full effect they will have on the individual.

From businesses, to schools , to everyday home activities technology is used on a daily bases in efficient ways. Businesses are able to run more efficiently and are able to cater to a large variety of people because of Online computer adds, television commercials, radio adds etc. Children in schools are learning better because they have faster resources such as ipad's and computers. One of the most controversial Technological devices right now are Cell phones and social Networks which are used by people all over the world of all different ages (facebook, Instagram, twitter , snap chat , etc.) .

Phone networks and social media founders are in two different lines of work that play hand and hand with each other. Social media has become used by millions of people who are able to access them obviously through devices like smart phones, ipads, tablets, and any other device that has internet access. When Phone companies are not selling products that allow easy access to these social networks that effects the sales of there phones; When phone companies networks are not running correctly or fast enough this effects the use of social media. Due to the fact these are 2 of the most popular inventions of this time people like Mark Zuckerberg are trying to work together with telecom carriers to expand internet access around the world. However Are telecom carriers willing to not only finance but put in the skill to further extend there internet services for the use of social media ?

Although there are positive effects caused by technology they don't always out weigh the negatives. Internet use and the use of social media has been the cause of bullying, suicide, harassment, bashing and false advertisement. People rely on there devices to do everyday tasks like finding directions, reading a book , writing, etc. because of this people are lacking skills they should have. These devices are also time consuming and often used not to learn but just to idle. instead of playing a sport people are watching sport on tv's, instead of reading books people are buying audio books online, instead of learning how to correctly spell people rely on spell checks using computers and smart phones, Besides the mental downplay this is having on everyday people , this is causing physical problems as well. Such as vision problems, obesity , being sleep deprived , migraines, carpel tunnel , and the list goes on. In todays society technology seems to be more important then ones health.

Technology is a " advance" in todays society and is known to be a glance into our future but what people don't realize are the set backs they also come with. yes they make things convenient and are easier to use then doing things the old fashion way but they are aslo dumbing down people causing them to lack common skill. Do we really need to worry about furthering these advances or finding solutions to the parts in which they lack ?

App Fees	Deadlines
Clark - $55	11/1/2016
Columbia - $85	1/1/2017
Drexel - $50	11/1/2016
Fordam - $70	11/1/2016
Georgia state $60	11/15/2016
NYU - $70	1/1/17
Smith - Free	1/15/2017
Spellman $35	11/15/2016
~~Sony $50~~	~~Free~~
Morrisville - $50	7/28/2017
Buffalo - $50	7/28/2017
Temple - $55	11/1/2016
Univ. of conne - $80	1/15/2017

* Oct 11, 12, 13, 14, 17 senior pictures retake

yearbook | 10/28/16
Senior pictures |

" How broke am I going to be after applying to college? "

Topic to teach: To explain the mass murder of millions of Jewish Americans specifically in auschwitz

Specific objective: To show the number of people tortured in Auschwitz concentration camp.

Required material: Projector, Computer, PowerPoint, me.

Procedure:

Slide 1: Title page with photograph of the entrance to Auschwitz.

Slide 2: Holocaust historical background and explanation of the main killing method which was the use of the gas chamber.

Slide 3: explanation of the gas zyklon b used in the gas chambers responsible for millions of deaths.

Slide 4: Examples of Zyklon b's physical effect on the human body.

Slide 5: Gas Chamber 1

Slide 6: Gas Chambers 2 and 3

Slide 7: Gas chambers 4 and 5

Slide 8: The Medical practices of Auschwitz and the doctor responsible, Dr.Mengele

Slide 9: Experiments on disabled performed in Auschwitz.

Slide 10: Experiments on women in Auschwitz

Slide 11: Museum Exhibits in the Auschwitz museum.

Slide 12: complete tour of Auschwitz grounds.

Slide 13: Work cited

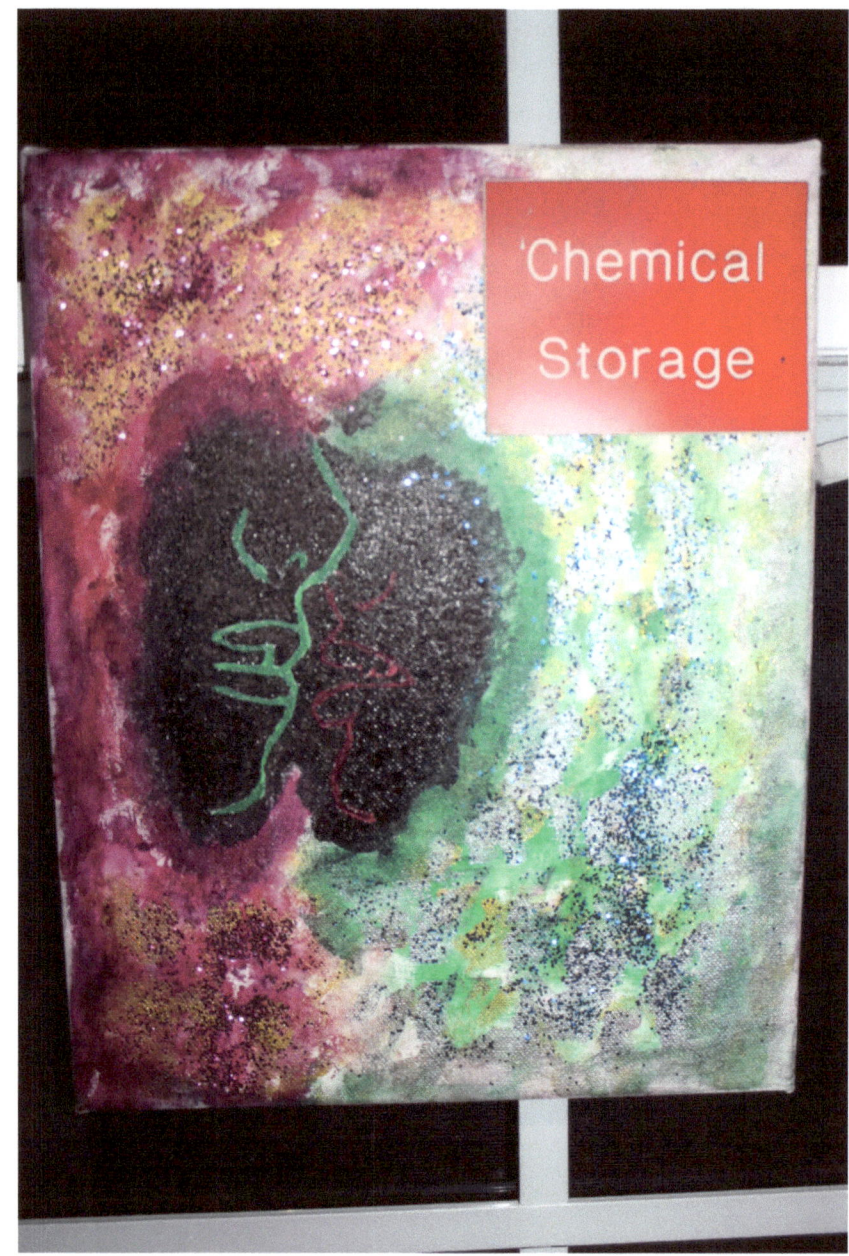

Title: Chemical storage

Artist: Mia Moore

Year: 2016

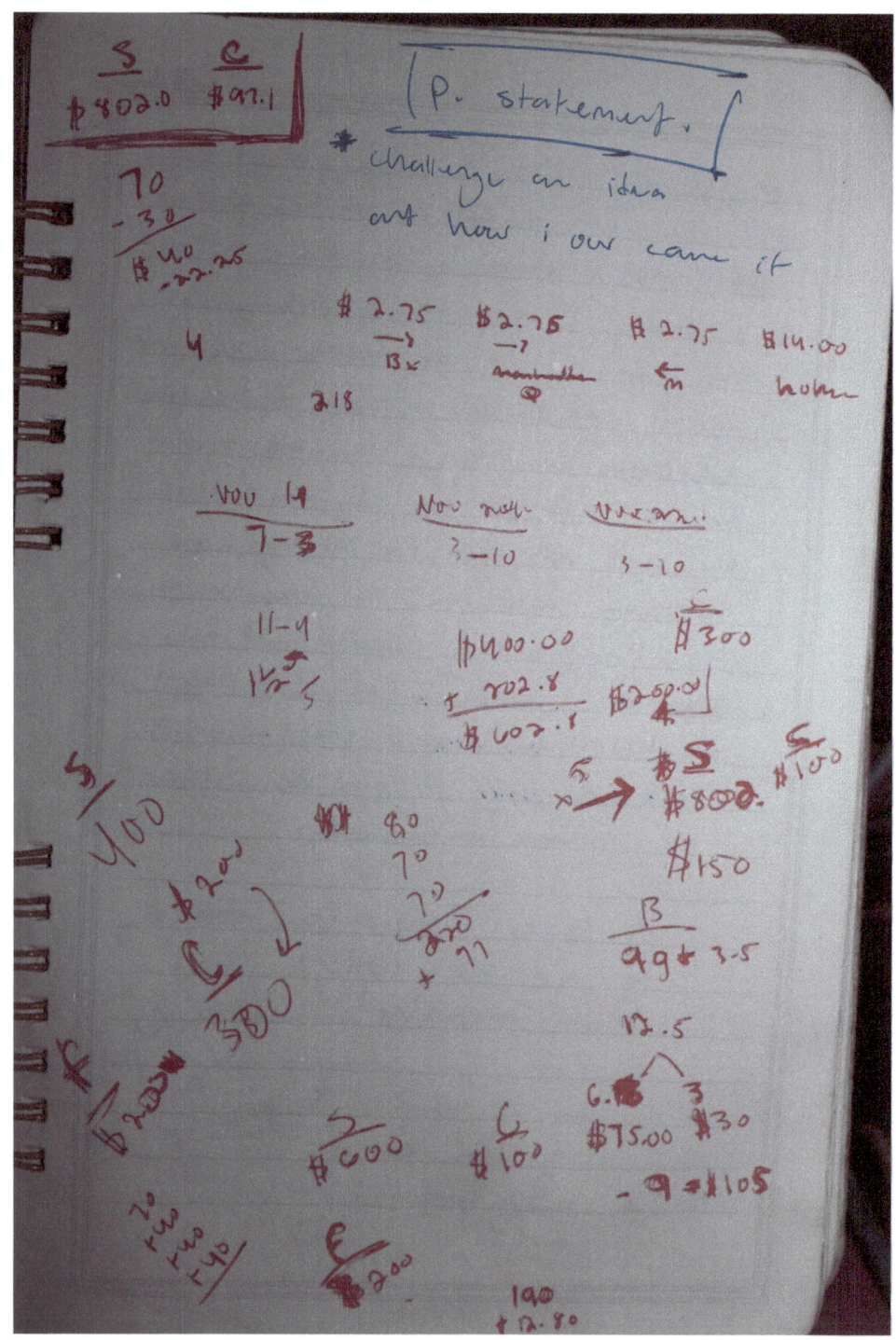

When you think you can avoid looking over your bank statement by writing things down yourself but it just ends up looking like this.

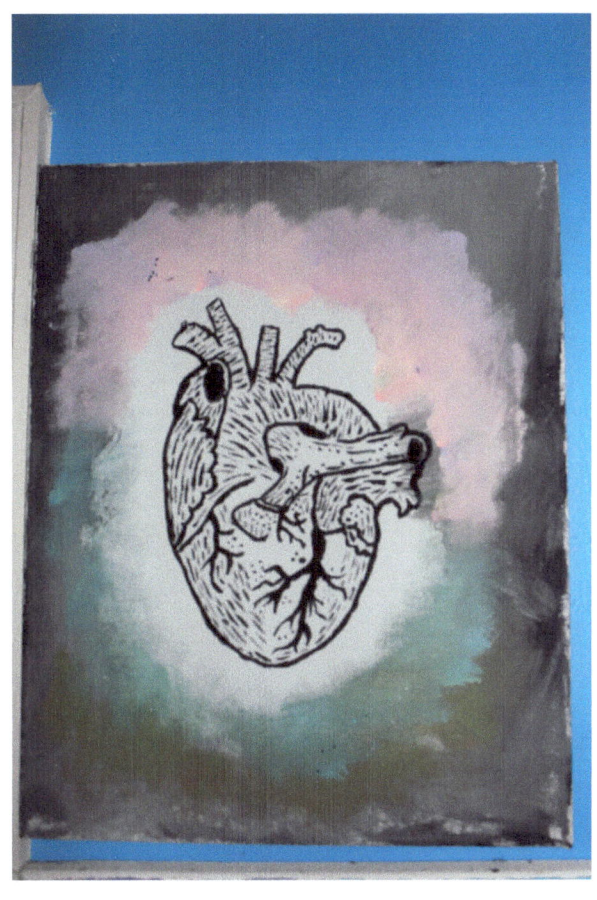

Title: Super Nova

Artist: Mia Moore

Year: 2016

Question: Why are you doing Q and A?

Answer: The real question is what valuable information could a 17 year old have to offer to the world. I feel like the world doesn't get to hear from kids and/or young adults because their opinions and struggles are deemed to have no importance or relevance to the real worlds; I am writing to assure or maybe even inform people that we are fully aware and just as much involved in the world as "adults". More importantly I want to emphasize we are not oblivious to what happens around us just because we have no voice.

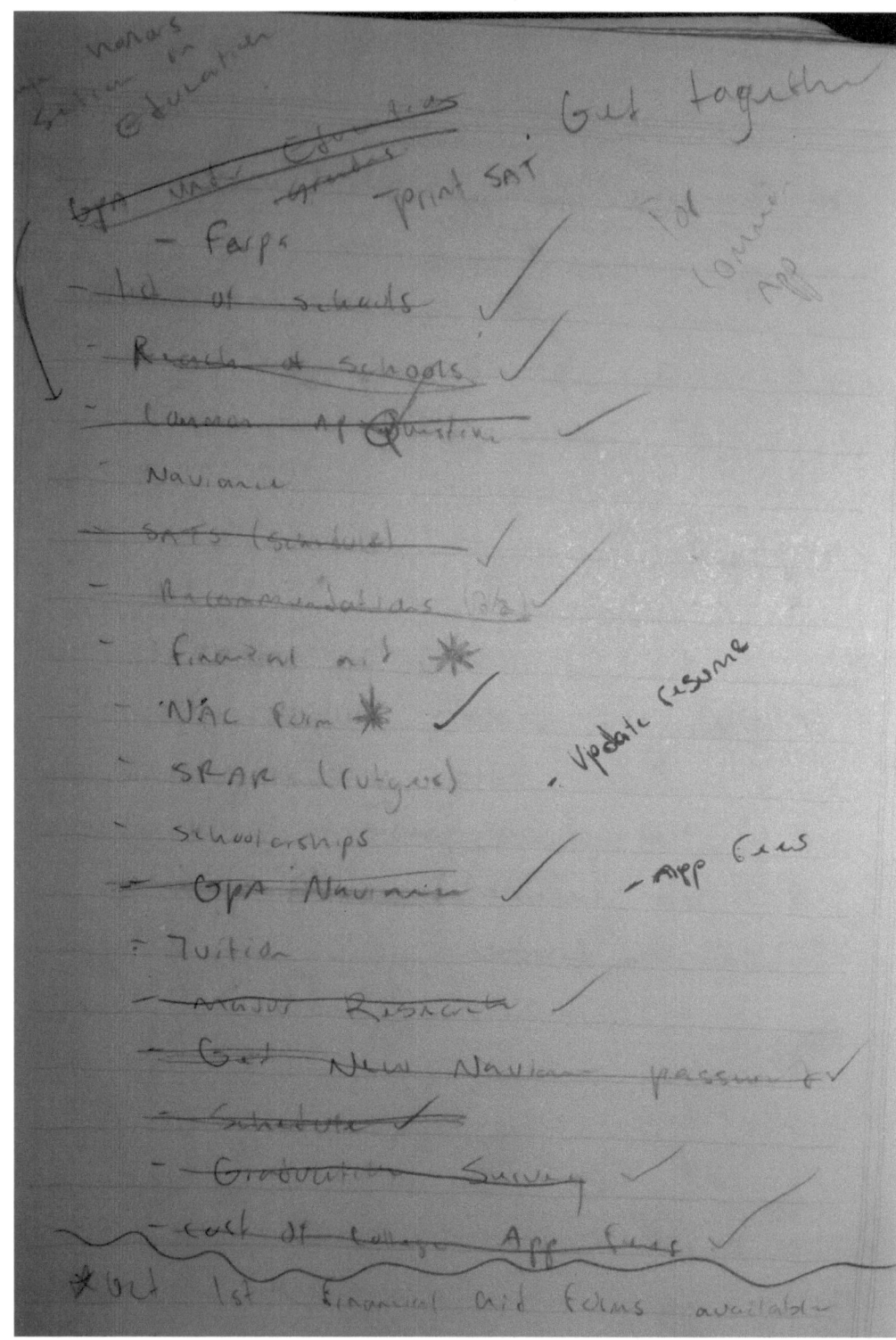

A simple list of steps you take to apply to college; it should be given to you but usually isn't, so your welcome.

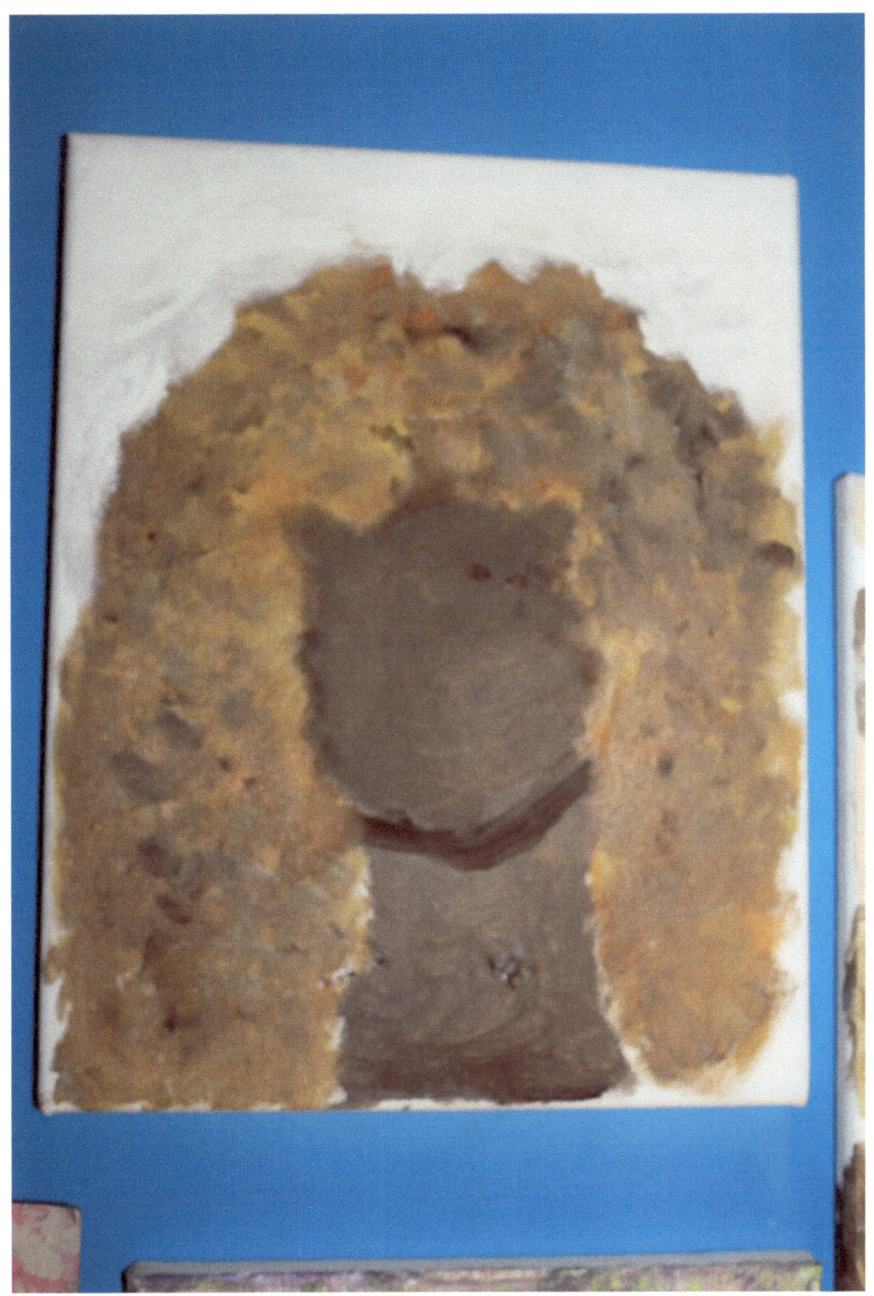

Title: *to be or not to be*

Artist: *Mia Moore*

Year: *2016*

" *Black hair, blond hair, real hair, fake hair, my hair.*"

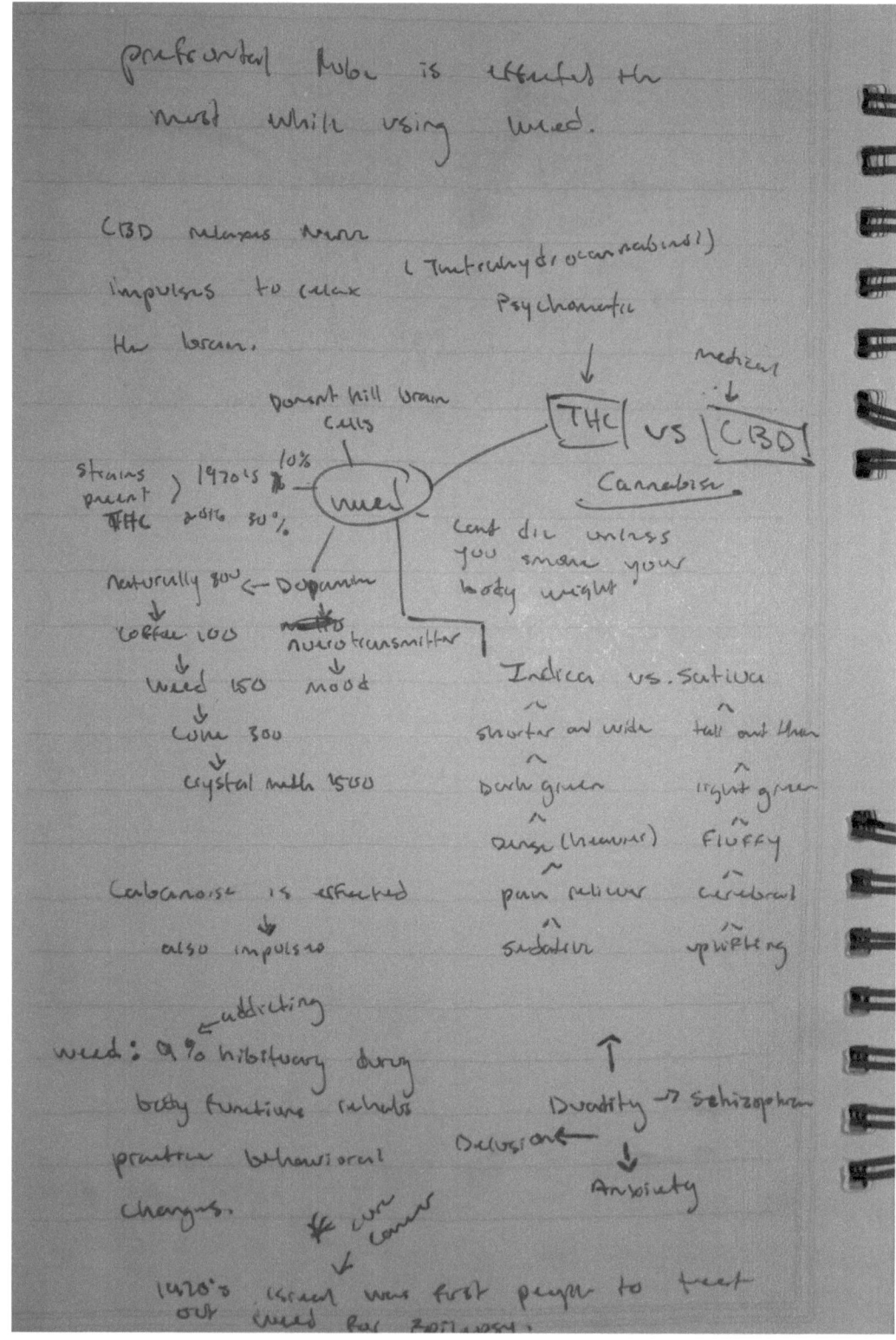

When someone tries to tell me that weed is killing my brain cells, so I have to quickly break it down.

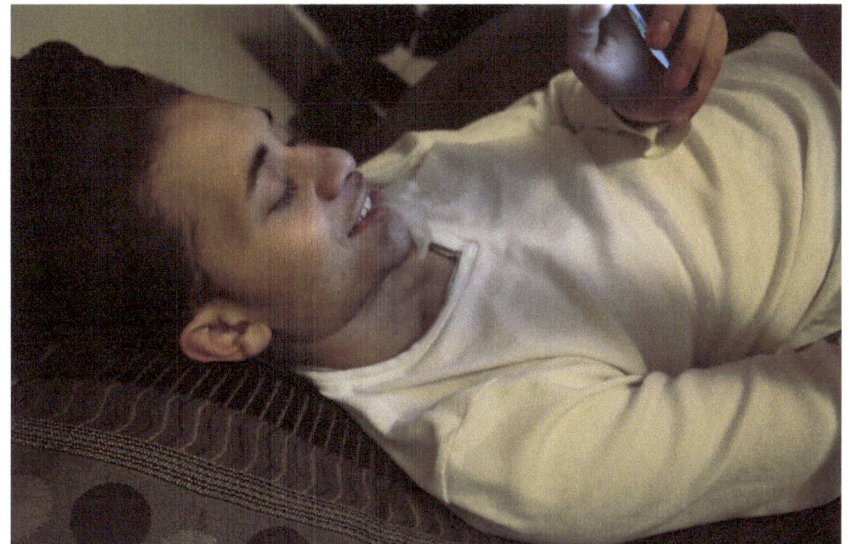

" Lets act like this is a normal picture and I'm not blowing gass."

other names for Gas

- loud

- candy

- glue

- dank

strands of gas

- Gorilla glue

- blood orange

- blue Dreams

- white OG

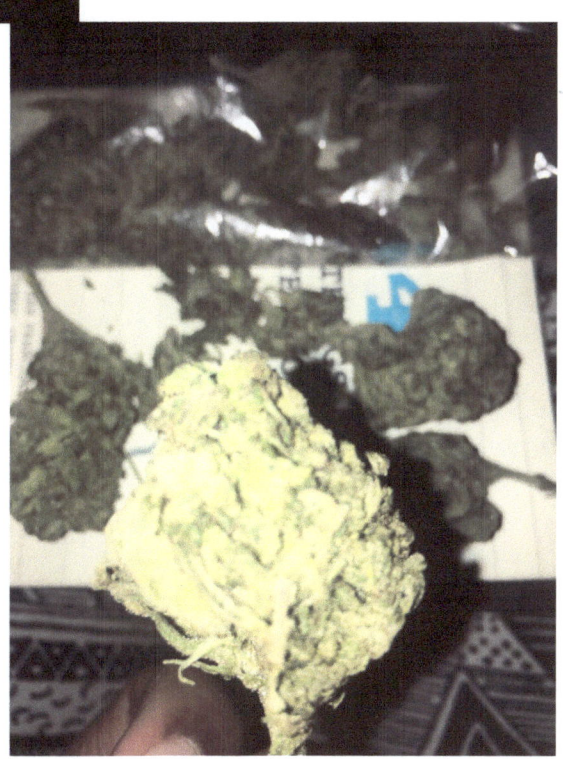

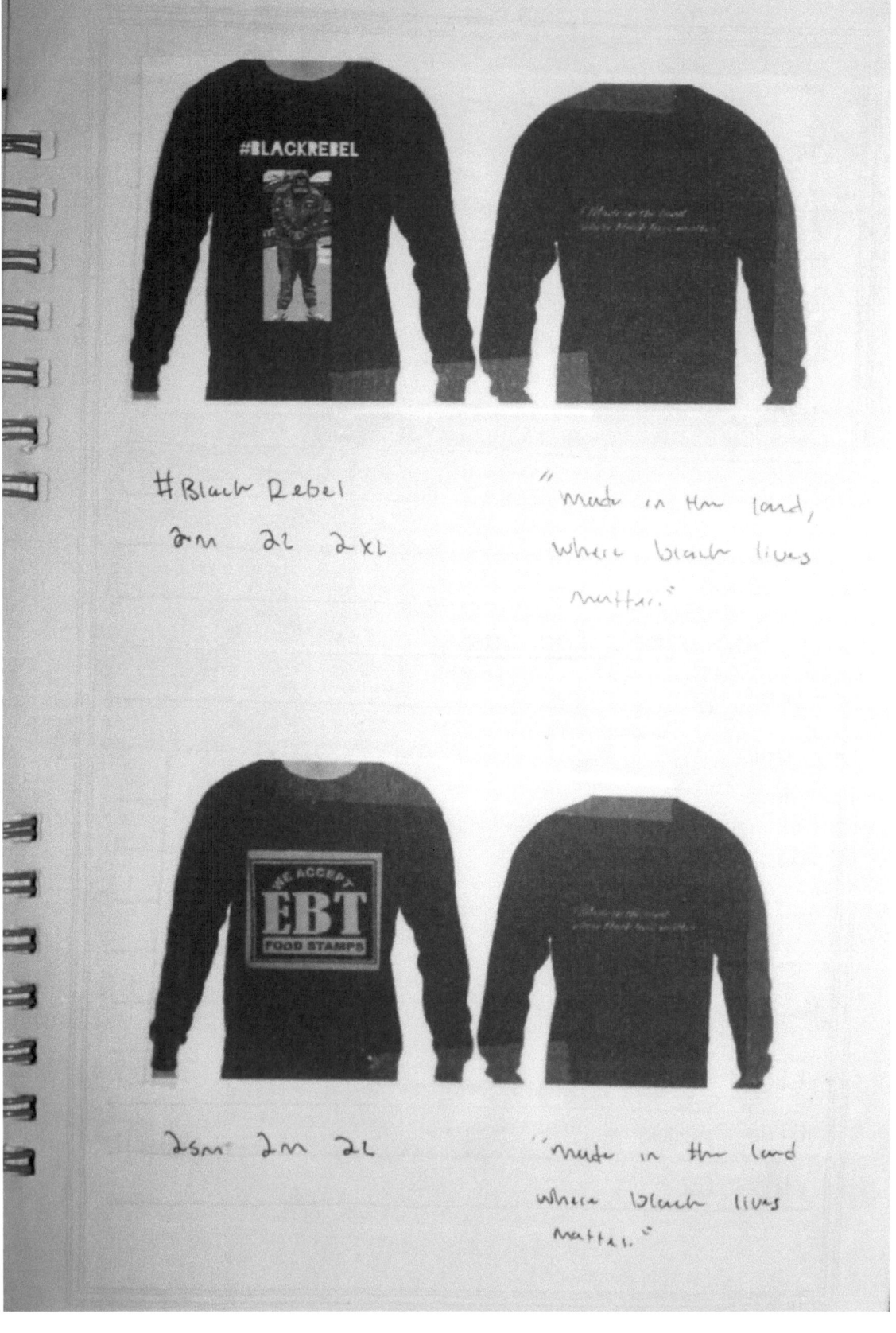

#Black Rebel
2m 2L 2XL

"made in the land,
where black lives
matter."

2sm 2m 2L

"made in the land
where black lives
matter."

Mia
2.11.15

Current events : The polio vaccine killed my father. But that's not a reason to oppose vaccines.

By Nuria Sheehan

Source : The Washington Post (http://www.washingtonpost.com/ posteverything/wp/2015/02/12/the-polio-vaccine-killed-my-father- but-thats-not-a-reason-to-oppóse-vaccines/?hpid=z11)

Summary : Sheehan's father was 1 in 5 million people who died from the polio vaccine. Although she was given the vaccine as a child it didn't affect her; however her father was infected with the virus. He spent less than a year in intensive car before he was completely paralyzed. Once her father died her mother tried to sue because before they were given the vaccine they were not told the possible risks; her mother didn't win the case.

Importance: I disagree with this article however, it is informal; there are a lot of vaccines that children have to get to do everyday things like go to school or participate in any type of programs with children. People rely on doctors and vaccines when doctors are not always sure of the outcome or effect a vaccine will have on a individual. Sheehan's father for example was 1 in 5 million people infected by the virus; although a very high percentage it is still possible for people to be infected by receiving this vaccine.

Broken (Adjective): having been fractured or damaged and no longer in one piece or in working order. At one point in time this would be the word I used to describe myself, until I was given a reason not to.. 2016 threw me multiple trials and tribulations but as a result I was given every reason Mentally, physically, spiritually, and academically to jump beyond those hurtles.

April 13th 2016 was day 1 of my continuous journey. While in my sophomore gym class, I was hit with a metal golf club instantly breaking my septum and left central incisor. I was taken into emergency surgery upon the arrival of my mother due to the fact I was a minor. One of my most vivid memories is sitting in the emergency room thinking about how I should be in choir rehearsal or sorting out my list of colleges my mother constantly questioned me about; but instead I was nearly conscious in the middle of an unfamiliar state, waiting to be drugged to numb the intense pain.

As a result of the accident I had a broken septum, a missing front tooth, whiplash and an intense concussion. Due to the procedures I was placed on pain medication and unable to attend school for 3 months. Post accident I was experiencing dizzy spells, extreme weight lost, black outs, difficulty breathing, and constant back problems. I received bone graphing replacing my center incisor tooth bone because it was too shattered to heal, put into physical therapy for my back problems, and placed on epilepsy medication for my intense migraines.

Missing 3 months of school placed me far behind my sophomore class, also considering I moved from New York City where I was being taught a completely different curriculum, taking classes for New York State graduation requirements not New Jersey. I was given no work the time I was out, given no home instruction, and was even given a problem have my absences medically excused. Besides all of the physical damage I faced, my spirit was beyond broken. I was at one of the lowest points in my life at 16 years old questioning what was going to become of my future. At that point is when I made the decision to not let the accident consume me but motivate me to push myself beyond playing victim and instead be a survivor of unfortunate circumstances.

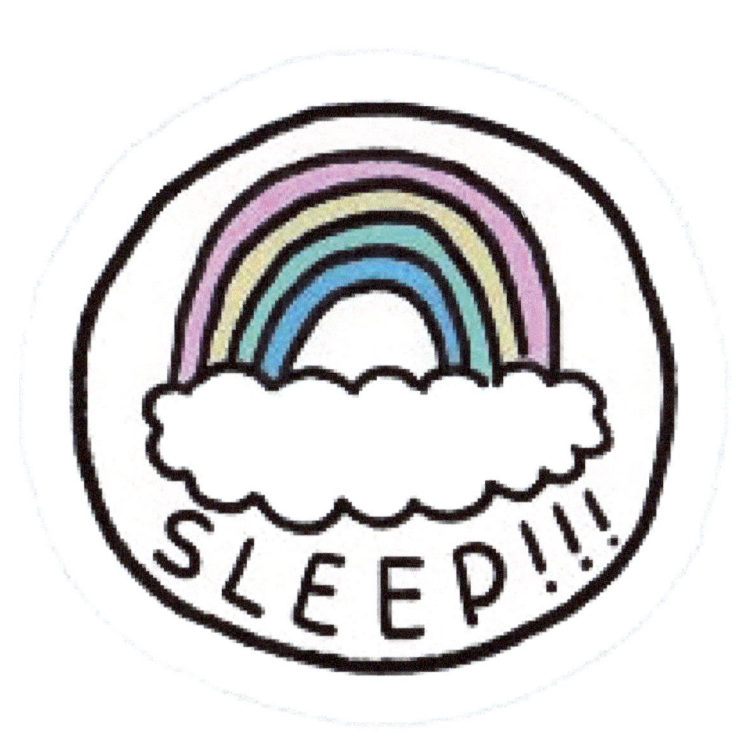

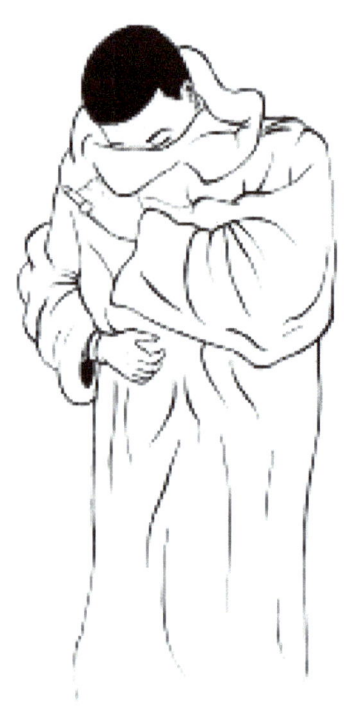

Since this is my last page
#FreeGuap2k17

- june 2017

Space for your thoughts :

Gmai : Miamoorehm@gmail

www.ingramcontent.com/pod-product-compliance
Lightning Source LLC
Chambersburg PA
CBHW050748180526
45159CB00003B/1389